The Picture Encyclopedia

Claire Llewellyn

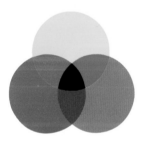

Scholastic Canada Ltd.

DK

A DK PUBLISHING BOOK

Project Editor Carey Combe
Art Editor Marcus James

Editors Patricia Grogan, Katherine Moss
Designers Sarah Cowley, Jacqueline Gooden, Joanna Hinton-Malivoire, Dean Price

US Editor Camela Decaire

DTP Designer Almudena Díaz

Managing Editor Jane Yorke
Managing Art Editor Chris Scollen

Picture Research James Clarke, Sally Hamilton
Picture Research Manager Melissa Albany

Production Josie Alabaster

Illustrators David Ashby, Chris Horsey, Janos Maffy

Consultants
Sally Whitton, Educational Consultant
Richard Woff, British Museum Education Service
Dale Buckton, DK Cartography

First Canadian Edition, 1997

Published in Canada
by Scholastic Canada Ltd.,
123 Newkirk Road, Richmond Hill,
Ontario, Canada L4C 3G5

Copyright © 1997 Dorling Kindersley Limited, London

Canadian Cataloguing in Publication Data
Llewellyn, Claire
The picture encyclopedia : a first A–Z
pictorial encyclopedia for younger readers
Includes index.
ISBN 0-590-24971-1
1. Children's encyclopedias and dictionaries I. Title.
AG5.L53 1997 j031 C97-930283-8

Published in Great Britain by Dorling Kindersley Ltd.

Color reproduction by Colourscan, Singapore
Printed and bound in Italy by Mondadori

Contents

About this book
4

A to Z entry pages

About this book

It's easy to find what you're looking for in **The Picture Encyclopedia**. The large heading of each main entry tells you what the page is about. Subjects are arranged alphabetically to help you quickly look up subjects that interest you.

Main entries
There are 145 exciting main entries to look up and learn about.

Alphabet
Use the alphabet at the top of the page to help you find your place in the encyclopedia.

Index
If you can't find the topic you are looking for, it may not be a main entry. Look it up in the index to find out which page it is on.

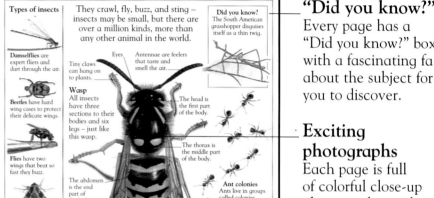

Insects
ABCDEFGH**I**JKLMNOPQRSTUVWXYZ

They crawl, fly, buzz, and sting – insects may be small, but there are over a million kinds, more than any other animal in the world.

Types of insects

Damselflies are expert fliers and dart through the air.

Beetles have hard wing cases to protect their delicate wings.

Flies have two wings that beat so fast they buzz.

Butterflies and moths have four patterned wings.

Did you know?
The South American grasshopper disguises itself as a thin twig.

Wasp
All insects have three sections to their bodies and six legs – just like this wasp.

Tiny claws can hang on to plants.

Eyes

Antennae are feelers that taste and smell the air.

The head is the first part of the body.

The thorax is the middle part of the body.

The abdomen is the end part of the body.

The six legs bend at the joints.

Wings

Ant colonies
Ants live in groups called colonies and share all the work to be done.

Growing up
Many insects change shape as they grow. This is called metamorphosis.

Ladybug egg

Larva

Pupa

Ladybug

1 A wormlike larva hatches from an egg. It feeds and grows.

2 The fully grown larva makes a hard case called a pupa around itself.

3 About a week later, the pupa splits open, and an adult ladybug crawls out.

86 Find out more ▶ Butterflies and moths 36 ▶ Insects of the world 87

"Did you know?"
Every page has a "Did you know?" box with a fascinating fact about the subject for you to discover.

Exciting photographs
Each page is full of colorful close-up photographs, and many feature step-by-step sequences.

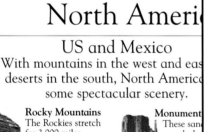

North Ameri[ca]
ABCDEFGHIJKLM**N**OPQ

Continents of the World

US and Mexico
With mountains in the west and eas[t], deserts in the south, North Americ[a has] some spectacular scenery.

Rocky Mountains
The Rockies stretch for 3,000 miles (4,800 km) down the western side of the US.

Monument[s]
These san[d]
rocks ha[ve]
carved
in the [...]
Desert[.]

The five Great Lakes make up the largest area of freshwater in the world.

States
1 VERMONT
2 NEW JERSEY
3 DELAWARE
4 MARYLAND
5 CONNECTICUT
6 NEW HAMPSHIRE
7 MASSACHUSETTS
8 RHODE ISLAND

WASHINGTON, MONTANA, NORTH DAKOTA, MINNESOTA, WISCONSIN, MICHIGAN, NEW Y[ORK], OREGON, IDAHO, WYOMING, SOUTH DAKOTA, NEBRASKA, IOWA, ILLINOIS, INDIANA, OHIO, PENNSYLVANIA, WASHINGTON D.C., NEVADA, UTAH, COLORADO, KANSAS, MISSOURI, KENTUCKY, VIRGINIA, NORTH CAROLINA, SOUTH CAROLINA, Death Valley, Grand Canyon, ARIZONA, NEW MEXICO, OKLAHOMA, ARKANSAS, TENNESSEE, MISSISSIPPI, ALABAMA, GEORGIA, Okefenokee Swamp, TEXAS, LOUISIANA, FLORIDA, EVERGLADES, Sonoran Desert, CALIFORNIA, ROCKY MOUNTAINS

U S

HAWAII

M E X I C O

MEXICO CITY

Collared lizard
This lizard manages to survive in the dry deserts.

Everglades
This vast tropical marsh in Florida is home to animals such as alligators.

Grand Canyon
This deep, rocky gorge has been cut out in Arizona by the Colorado River.

Death Valley
Death Valley in California is the hottest, driest place in the whole of North America.

Sonoran Desert
This desert lies between the US and Mexico. It is famous for its giant cacti.

Okefenokee Swamp
This freshwater swamp in southern Georgia is a safe refuge for wildlife.

104 Find out more ▶ Desert animals 45 ▶ Water 146

Picture cross-references
At the bottom of each page, you will find out where to look for more information on related subjects.

Illustrated maps
Large picture maps on many pages help you learn about different parts of the world.

Subentries
Every page has several subentries giving you more information about the main subject. You can find these by using the index.

Find out more
Each main entry falls into one of five key subject areas, indicated by the symbol in the top left-hand corner of the page. The picture cross-references at the bottom of the page offer suggestions for related entries to look up.

World of Nature
This subject area covers the natural world, from birds to polar lands.

Continents of the World
Information about regions, countries, and continents is found in this key subject area.

Life in the Past
Learn all about ancient civilizations and prehistoric life in this key subject area.

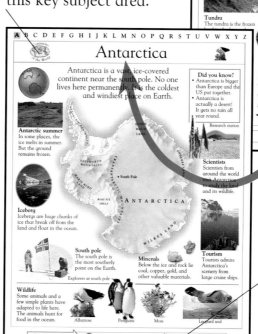

The picture cross-references guide you to other main entries.

Life Today
If you look up topics in this key subject area, you will find out about everything from transportation to sports.

Science and Technology
This key subject area includes everything in the world of science, from the human body to space travel.

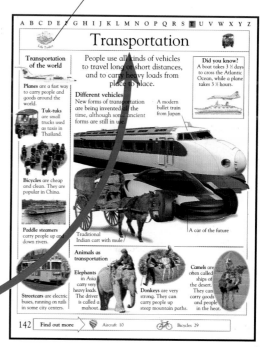

Continents of the World

Africa

Northern Africa

Northern Africa is one of the hottest parts of the world. It is made up of mountains, rain forests, and a great, sweeping desert.

Atlas Mountains
These mountains form a high wall between the Sahara Desert and the wetter land on the coast.

Rain forest
Rain forest grows near the equator, where there is heavy rain.

Hoggar Mountains
These red mountains rise up out of the Sahara Desert.

Nile River
The muddy banks of the Nile make fertile farmland.

Ethiopian Highlands
The Ethiopian Highlands are hot, dry scrubland. Farming is very difficult here.

Map labels

RABAT • — ALGIERS • — TUNIS •
MOROCCO
ATLAS MOUNTAINS
TUNISIA
EL AAIUN • — • TRIPOLI
Suez Canal
WESTERN SAHARA
ALGERIA
LIBYA
CAIRO •
Nile River
S A H A R A   D E S E R T
EGYPT
NOUAKCHOTT •
MAURITANIA
HOGGAR MOUNTAINS
MALI
NIGER
KHARTOUM •
ERITREA
ASMARA •
SENEGAL
GAMBIA
GUINEA BISSAU
BAMAKO •
OUAGADOUGOU — NIAMEY •
CHAD
Lake Chad
SUDAN
DJIBOUTI
DJIBOUTI
GUINEA
BURKINA
N'DJAMENA •
ETHIOPIAN HIGHLANDS
SIERRA LEONE
IVORY COAST
TOGO BENIN
NIGERIA
ABUJA •
ADDIS ABABA •
LIBERIA
GHANA
ACCRA — LOME
PORTO-NOVO
CENTRAL AFRICAN REPUBLIC
ETHIOPIA
CAMEROON
BANGUI •
SOMALIA
YAOUNDE •
MOGADISHU •

Capital cities
1 DAKAR
2 BANJUI
3 BISSAU
4 CONAKRY
5 FREETOWN
6 MONROVIA
7 YAMOUSSOUKRO

Sahara Desert
The Sahara Desert has burning hot days and freezing cold nights. Winds blow the sand into dunes.

Lake Chad
Lake Chad is now shrinking as the rivers that feed it are drying up.

Fennec fox
The fennec fox lives in the desert. Its huge ears give off heat, cooling the fox down.

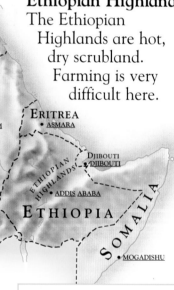

Did you know?
- The Sahara Desert is the largest desert in the world.
- At 4,145 miles (6,670 km), the Nile is the longest river in the world.

Find out more → Deserts 46   Rivers and lakes 119

Find out more

Each main entry falls into one of five key subject areas, indicated by the symbol in the top left-hand corner of the page. The picture cross-references at the bottom of the page offer suggestions for related entries to look up.

Life in the Past
Learn all about ancient civilizations and prehistoric life in this key subject area.

World of Nature
This subject area covers the natural world, from birds to polar lands.

Continents of the World
Information about regions, countries, and continents is found in this key subject area.

Polar lands

A B C D E F G H I J K L M N O **P** Q R S T U V W X Y Z

World of Nature

The polar lands lie around the north and south poles. The frozen ground and icy climate make them a hard place for plants to grow.

Ice field
A lot of the land in the polar regions is covered by huge sheets of ice, called ice fields.

Glaciers flow from the ice fields.
Glaciers are rivers of ice that move slowly down mountain slopes.

Antarctica
No one lives in the Antarctic, but scientists visit to study the land and its wildlife.

Polar plants

Mosses grow in thick cushions. This protects them from icy winds.

The **Arctic wormwood** stores food in its roots to help it survive.

Grasses grow quickly in the spring when there are long periods of daylight.

Primroses have long roots to help them survive.

Tundra
The tundra is the frozen

Life in the Arctic
People have lived in the Arctic for thousands of years. They have had to adapt their lifestyle to the harsh climate.

Winter coat
Dog-pulled sleds make it possible to move goods across the ice.

Warm clothes are made from animal skins.

Husky

Sled

Fleabane grows only for a few weeks in the Arctic summer.

Find out more		
Antarctica 19		Polar animals 111

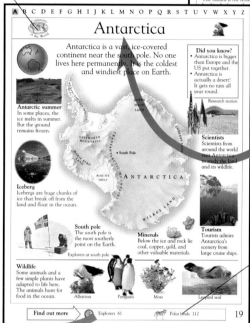

Antarctica

A B **C** D E F G H I **J** K L M N O P Q R S T U V W X Y Z

Continents of the World

Antarctica is a vast, ice-covered continent near the south pole. No one lives here permanently. It is the coldest and windiest place on Earth.

Did you know?
• Antarctica is bigger than Europe and the US put together.
• Antarctica is actually a desert. It gets no rain all year round.

Antarctic summer
In some places, the ice melts in summer. But the ground remains frozen.

Research station

Scientists
Scientists from around the world visit Antarctica to study the land and its wildlife.

Iceberg
Icebergs are huge chunks of ice that break off from the land and float in the ocean.

South pole
The south pole is the most southerly point on the Earth.

Explorers at south pole

Minerals
Below the ice and rock lie coal, copper, gold, and other valuable materials.

Tourism
Tourists admire Antarctica's scenery from large cruise ships.

Wildlife
Some animals and a few simple plants have adapted to life here. The animals hunt for food in the ocean.

Albatross

Penguins

Moss

Leopard seal

Find out more			
	Explorers 61	Polar lands 112	19

The picture cross-references guide you to other main entries.

Life Today
If you look up topics in this key subject area, you will find out about everything from transportation to sports.

Explorers

A B C D **E** F G H I J K L M N O P Q R S T U V W X Y Z

Life in the Past

Travelers

For thousands of years people have explored the world, hoping to find fertile farmland, fine goods, and riches.

Round Earth
In 1519 a famous Spanish explorer, Magellan, sailed around the world – and proved that it was round.

Pacific islanders were the first to cross the Pacific Ocean.

Sailing ship
Starting in the 1400's, European sailors explored the world in fast, sturdy ships like this one.

The **Vikings** sailed to the south to find fertile farmland.

Viking helmet

Four masts for large sails

Sailors spotted land from the crow's nest.

Ship's compass

Merchants explored the route between China and Europe to trade in silk.

Arabs traveled in the 13th century to trade and find new lands.

Room for cargo, food, and water

Finding the way
Explorers used the sun, stars, and instruments to find their way.

Sextant

Goods
Explorers brought home new foods and riches from around the world.

Jade

Did you know?
Before the 1520's, most people thought the world was flat!

Backstaff

Telescope

Cloves

Cinnamon

Pineapple

Columbus, Spanish explorer, crossed the Atlantic Ocean using an astrolabe.

Find out more			
	Vikings 145	Ships and boats 127	61

Science and Technology
This key subject area includes everything in the world of science, from the human body to space travel.

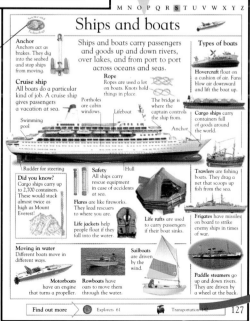

Ships and boats

M N O P Q R **S** T U V W X Y Z

Science and Technology

Anchor
Anchors act as brakes. They dig into the seabed and stop ships from moving.

Ships and boats carry passengers and goods up and down rivers, over lakes, and from port to port across oceans and seas.

Types of boats

Hovercraft float on a cushion of air. Fans blow air downward and lift the boat up.

Cruise ship
All boats do a particular kind of job. A cruise ship gives passengers a vacation at sea.

Rope
Ropes are used a lot on boats. Knots hold things in place.

Portholes are cabin windows.

Lifeboat

The bridge is where the captain controls the ship from.

Cargo ships carry containers full of goods around the world.

Swimming pool

Anchor

Rudder for steering

Hull

Did you know?
Cargo ships carry up to 2,700 containers. These would stack almost twice as high as Mount Everest.

Safety
All ships carry rescue equipment in case of accidents at sea.

Flares are like fireworks. They lead rescuers to where you are.

Life rafts are used to carry passengers if their boat sinks.

Life jackets help people float if they fall into the water.

Trawlers are fishing boats. They drag a net that scoops up fish from the sea.

Frigates have missiles on board to strike enemy ships in times of war.

Moving in water
Different boats move in different ways.

Motorboats have an engine that turns a propeller.

Rowboats have oars to move them through the water.

Sailboats are driven by the wind.

Paddle steamers go up and down rivers. They are driven by a wheel at the back.

Find out more			
	Explorers 61	Transportation 142	127

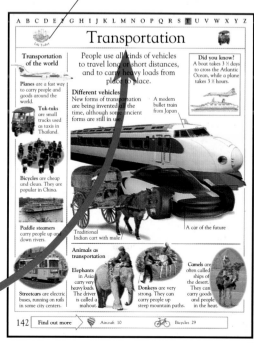

Transportation

A B C D E F **G** H I J K L M N O P Q R S **T** U V W X Y Z

Life Today

Transportation of the world

People use all kinds of vehicles to travel long or short distances, and to carry heavy loads from place to place.

Did you know?
A boat takes 3½ days to cross the Atlantic Ocean, while a plane takes 3½ hours.

Planes are a fast way to carry people and goods around the world.

Different vehicles
New forms of transportation are being invented all the time, although some ancient forms are still in use.

A modern bullet train from Japan

Tuk-tuks are small trucks used as taxis in Thailand.

Bicycles are cheap and clean. They are popular in China.

A car of the future

Paddle steamers carry people up and down rivers.

Traditional Indian cart with mule

Animals as transportation

Elephants in Asia carry very heavy loads. The driver is called a mahout.

Streetcars are electric buses, running on rails in some city centers.

Donkeys are very strong. They can carry people up steep mountain paths.

Camels are often called ships of the desert. They can carry goods and people in the heat.

142	Find out more	Aircraft 10	Bicycles 29

5

Continents of the World

Africa

Northern Africa
Northern Africa is one of the hottest parts of the world. It is made up of mountains, rain forests, and a great, sweeping desert.

Atlas Mountains
These mountains form a high wall between the Sahara Desert and the wetter land on the coast.

Hoggar Mountains
These red mountains rise up out of the Sahara Desert.

Nile River
The muddy banks of the Nile make fertile farmland.

Rain forest
Rain forest grows near the equator, where there is heavy rain.

Ethiopian Highlands
The Ethiopian Highlands are hot, dry scrubland. Farming is very difficult here.

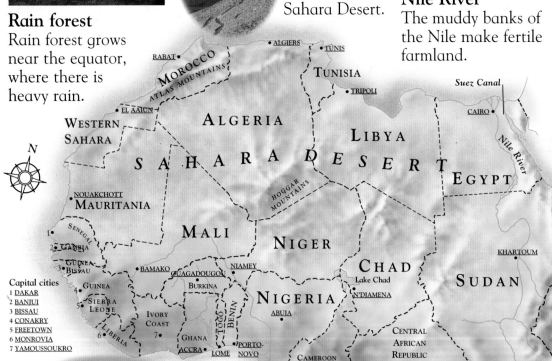

N

* ALGIERS
RABAT •
• TUNIS
MOROCCO
ATLAS MOUNTAINS
TUNISIA
• TRIPOLI
Suez Canal
• EL AAIUN
CAIRO •
WESTERN SAHARA
ALGERIA
LIBYA
Nile River
EGYPT
S A H A R A   D E S E R T
• NOUAKCHOTT
MAURITANIA
HOGGAR MOUNTAINS
MALI
ERITREA
• ASMARA
1 • SENEGAL
NIGER
KHARTOUM •
2 • GAMBIA
• BAMAKO
• OUAGADOUGOU
• NIAMEY
CHAD
SUDAN
DJIBOUTI • DJIBOUTI
3 • GUINEA BISSAU
BURKINA
Lake Chad
Capital cities
4 •
GUINEA
• N'DJAMENA
ETHIOPIAN HIGHLANDS
1 DAKAR
SIERRA LEONE
NIGERIA
• ADDIS ABABA
2 BANJUL
5 •
IVORY COAST
BENIN
ABUJA •
3 BISSAU
LIBERIA
TOGO
CENTRAL AFRICAN REPUBLIC
ETHIOPIA
4 CONAKRY
6 •
GHANA
• PORTO-NOVO
S O M A L I A
5 FREETOWN
7 •
ACCRA •
LOME
CAMEROON
• BANGUI
6 MONROVIA
• YAOUNDE
• MOGADISHU
7 YAMOUSSOUKRO

Fennec fox
The fennec fox lives in the desert. Its huge ears give off heat, cooling the fox down.

Did you know?
- The Sahara Desert is the largest desert in the world.
- At 4,145 miles (6,670 km), the Nile is the longest river in the world.

Sahara Desert
The Sahara Desert has burning hot days and freezing cold nights. Winds blow the sand into dunes.

Lake Chad
Lake Chad is now shrinking as the rivers that feed it are drying up.

Find out more ➤ Deserts 46 — Rivers and lakes 119

Continents of the World

Africa

Southern Africa
Southern Africa's thick rain forests, dry deserts, and rolling grasslands are home to a huge variety of animals and plants.

Mount Kilimanjaro
Although this ancient volcano lies close to the equator, it is always covered in snow.

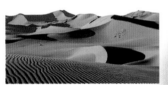

Congo rain forest
The Congo rain forest is home to a huge variety of wildlife.

Great Rift Valley
This huge valley was formed millions of years ago. It is a land of lakes and volcanoes.

Namib Desert
This desert has towering sand dunes. It contains diamonds and precious metals.

Map labels:
MALABO, EQUATORIAL GUINEA, LIBREVILLE, GABON, CONGO, Congo River, BRAZZAVILLE, CABINDA, KINSHASA, ZAIRE, UGANDA, KAMPALA, KENYA, NAIROBI, RWANDA, KIGALI, BUJUMBURA, BURUNDI, Lake Victoria, SERENGETI PLAIN, Mount Kilimanjaro, DODOMA, TANZANIA, LUANDA, ANGOLA, Zambezi River, ZAMBIA, LUSAKA, LILONGWE, MALAWI, MOZAMBIQUE, HARARE, Victoria Falls, ZIMBABWE, NAMIBIA, WINDHOEK, NAMIB DESERT, BOTSWANA, GABORONE, MADAGASCAR, PRETORIA, MAPUTO, MBABANE, SWAZILAND, Vaal River, BLOEMFONTEIN, MASERU, LESOTHO, SOUTH AFRICA, CAPE TOWN, Table Mountain

N (compass)

Victoria Falls
This dramatic waterfall drops over a steep cliff in the Zambezi River.

Baobab tree
These trees survive dry weather by storing water inside their trunks.

Serengeti Plain
This plain is a vast area of grassland. Huge herds of grazing animals live here.

Did you know?
- The Great Rift Valley is a huge crack in the Earth's crust.
- At 19,340 ft (5,895 m), Mt. Kilimanjaro is the highest mountain in Africa.

Table Mountain
This flat-topped mountain is often hidden by a cloud that locals call the "tablecloth."

Wildlife
No two zebras are exactly the same. Their stripes camouflage them, and help confuse their enemies.

Find out more Grassland animals 76   Rain forests 114

Continents of the World

Africa: culture

Culture

Textiles are bold and colorful. This carpet was made in Morocco.

Dance and music are an important and popular part of African village life.

Crafts, such as wood carving, are practiced all over Africa.

Africa is home to millions of people. Most of them live in small villages and farm the land, but more and more are moving to the cities.

Market

Many towns in Africa have a daily market, where people gather to buy and sell goods and chat with friends.

Minerals
There are gold and diamond mines in southern and western Africa.

Tourism

Thousands of tourists visit Africa to see its magnificent landscape and wildlife.

Buyer

Farming

Many Africans still use traditional farming methods to grow food crops such as corn.

Farmer in Zimbabwe

Corn

Wheat couscous

Towns and cities

Cities in Africa are growing quickly as people leave their villages to look for work.

Cairo

Village houses are made with a mix of dried mud and straw baked hard in the sun.

Shantytowns are home to the very poor. The shelters have no water or electricity.

Did you know?

In Chad, more than 40,000 people have to share one doctor.

Find out more Towns and cities 140 Dance 44

Science and Technology

Air

Air is a mixture of gases that swirl around the Earth. We cannot see, smell, or taste air, but it contains the oxygen we need to live and breathe.

Air pressure
Barometers measure air pressure – the weight of air pressing on the Earth.

Barometer

Air resistance
Air pushes against a parachute as it falls to Earth, and this slows it down.

Gases in air
Humans breathe in oxygen and breathe out carbon dioxide. Plants take in carbon dioxide and put oxygen back into the air.

Air power
Hovercraft float above the sea on a cushion of air.

Air resistance makes parachutes fall slowly.

Canopy

Harness

Parachutist

Air currents
Air currents are pockets of moving air.

People use air currents for sports such as hang-gliding.

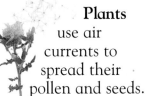

Birds use air currents to help them fly.

Plants use air currents to spread their pollen and seeds.

Wind power
Wind is moving air. It can turn wind turbines, which make electricity.

Did you know?
Without air, the sky would look black even during the day!

Mountain air
On mountain peaks, the air is cold and contains less oxygen.

Wind speed
People use the Beaufort scale when they want to measure the speed and strength of wind.

Light air – force 1

Gentle breeze – force 3

Strong breeze – force 6

Moderate gale – force 7

Strong gale – force 9

Aircraft

The fastest way to travel is by air. Aircraft can carry people around the world in just a few hours.

Passenger plane

Planes today are often used to carry passengers long distances. This one can carry more than 100 people.

Flying instruments

The fuselage is the body of the plane, where passengers sit.

Cockpit
The cockpit contains the computers and controls used by the pilot.

Streamlined shape

Cockpit

Light aluminum body

Jet engines power the plane forward.

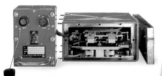

Wing flaps help the plane slow down and turn in the air.

Types of aircraft

Helicopters have spinning blades called rotors.

Hot-air balloons fly because hot air is lighter than cold air.

Did you know?
The long, pointed nose of the Concorde "droops" so that the pilot has a clear view for landing!

Wheels
These fold up inside the plane during flight.

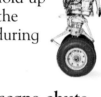

Black box
This records all the details of an aircraft's flight.

Escape chute
Air-filled chutes are the emergency exits from an airplane.

Airships are filled with helium gas, which is lighter than air.

Airport
Planes take off and land at airports. Cargo is brought here, and passengers wait for their flight.

Food and drink is loaded onto a plane.

Staff direct takeoff and landing from the control tower.

Passengers wait in the terminal.

Seaplanes have pontoons. They can land on water.

Gliders are towed up into the sky. They have no engine and glide on air currents.

Find out more Inventions 88   Transportation 142

World of Nature

Amphibians

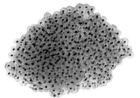

Breathing
Frogs breathe through their skin when underwater, but use their lungs on dry land.

Amphibians are animals like frogs and newts, which live partly in freshwater and partly on land. They lay their eggs in water.

Nostrils

Damp skin

Strong back legs for hopping and swimming

Large eyes look for insects.

Webbed feet move like paddles in the water.

Frog
The red-eyed tree frog is one of 4,000 different amphibians. Its body is well adapted to life both in water and on land.

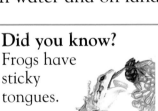

Did you know?
Frogs have sticky tongues.

They flick them out to snag prey.

Deadly color
Some amphibians, like this frog, are poisonous. Their bright colors warn other animals not to eat them.

Golden poison-arrow frog

Growing up
Amphibians change their shape as they grow. This is called metamorphosis.

1 Large groups of frog eggs are called spawn.

2 Each egg grows into a tiny tadpole that takes in air through its gills.

Gills

3 The tadpole grows legs and loses its tail.

Common frog

4 The grown-up frog breathes with lungs.

Other amphibians

Marbled newt

Ornate horned toad

Fire salamander

Newts have a long, thin body like a lizard.

Toads look like frogs, but have bumpy skin.

Salamanders spend most of their time on land.

Find out more ➤ Rain forest animals 113   River animals 118

Life in the Past

Ancient China

China was formed more than 2,000 years ago. Powerful emperors kept China isolated from the rest of the world.

Chinese inventions

Compasses were used at sea on Chinese ships.

Wheelbarrows were invented about 2,000 years ago.

An **earthquake detector** felt the slightest shaking of the Earth.

Paper was made from straw, rags, and water.

Dragon
The dragon was an important symbol of strength and goodness. It was the emperor's symbol, too.

Colorful material

Scales of a fish

Dragon costumes were worn at important festivals.

Ears of a bull

Demon eyes

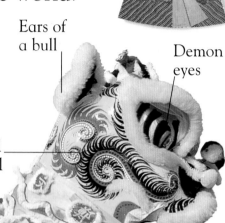

Silk robe
Rich people wore beautiful robes made of expensive silk.

Dragon seal
Emperors used this seal to sign important papers.

Entertainment
The ancient Chinese loved drama and playing games, such as chess.

Chess pieces

Gambling counters

Actor

Did you know?
The Chinese used kites in the shapes of dragons to frighten enemies in battle.

Emperor
Ancient China was ruled by emperors. The royal family was called a dynasty.

The Kangxi emperor ruled China 300 years ago.

The tomb of the first emperor was guarded by a huge army of life-size clay soldiers.

The first emperor completed the Great Wall of China. It is still standing today.

Find out more ▷ Asia: culture 21   Inventions 88

Life in the Past

Ancient Egypt

Writing
Egyptian writing was made up of rows of pictures called hieroglyphs.

About 5,000 years ago, Egypt was one of the most powerful and advanced countries in the world.

Pyramid
The pyramids are the tombs of dead pharaohs. They were built with millions of heavy stone blocks.

Pyramids pointed to heaven.

Pharaohs were buried inside.

Nile River
Egyptian farmers grew plenty of food on the banks of the Nile.

The Great Pyramid at Giza

Arts and crafts

Pottery jars and pots were made from river mud.

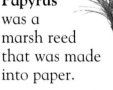

Pictures of everyday life were often painted on rich people's tombs.

Papyrus was a marsh reed that was made into paper.

Metal, such as bronze, was used to make items like mirrors and razors.

Lucky charm   Pendant

Jewelry was worn by the wealthy. It was often made of gold.

Toys
Egyptian children played with balls and spinning tops.

Afterlife
Egyptians believed in life after death. So dead bodies were carefully preserved. These are called mummies.

Cats were very important in Egypt. They were preserved, too.

Did you know?
Dead pharaohs were buried with food and drink to help them on their journey into the next life!

Pharaoh
The kings and queens of Egypt were called pharaohs. They were thought to be gods.

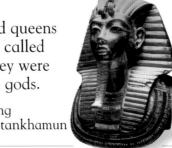

Queen Nefertiti   King Tutankhamun

Find out more ▶   Africa 6   Buildings 35

Life in the Past

Ancient Greece

Gods
The Greeks had many gods. Zeus was king of the gods.

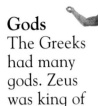
Zeus

Temple
The Greeks built wonderful stone temples to their gods. The Parthenon is 2,500 years old.

The ancient Greeks lived more than 2,500 years ago, but many of their ideas are still important to us today.

Stone carvings

Mirror
This beautiful bronze mirror is decorated with a picture of Aphrodite, the goddess of beauty.

Marble columns

Carved columns

Arts and crafts

Theater was very popular. The Greeks wrote many plays.

Pottery vases were made of red clay, and then decorated.

Toys for children were made of painted clay.

Metals were made into statues and jewelry.

Gold earring

Family life
Ancient Greek families were very close. Marriages were often arranged.

Food
Many ancient Greeks ate bread, eggs, fresh fish, and figs.

Fresh figs

Fresh fish

Education
Boys went to school. They studied music, reading, and writing.

Two boys reading books are pictured on this pitcher.

Musical instruments

Socrates was a famous teacher and thinker. His ideas are still read today.

Statue of Socrates

Olympics
The Greeks loved sports. They invented the Olympic Games.

Painting of athletes

Did you know?
Masks and platform shoes were worn in ancient Greek theater when actors played the parts of gods.

14

Find out more ➤ Religions 115   Sports of the world 136

World of Nature

Animal families

Every animal has a different kind of family life. Some animals live alone and come together only to mate, others live in family groups.

Did you know?
Male black widow spiders are often eaten by their bigger female mate!

Lion
Lions live in family groups called prides. They share out the food between them.

Lionesses do most of the hunting.

Male lions protect the group.

Domestic cat
Unlike lions, domestic cats live alone.

All the females look after the cubs.

Family groups

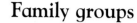

Humans often live in a small group called a nuclear family.

Meerkats live in a large group called an extended family.

Sharks live on their own, coming together briefly only to mate.

Watching over baby
Male **rheas** take care of the female's eggs, then look after their babies for a few months.

Scorpions carry their babies on their backs.

Baby bats are taken care of in one large group called a nursery.

Baby **birds** are fed by both parents until they leave the nest.

Flycatcher

Some **fish** protect their babies by carrying them in their mouths.

Cichlid

Find out more Animal homes 16 Living things 91

World of Nature

Animal homes

Some animals make homes, others find temporary shelters. Whether animals live alone or in groups, their homes protect them from danger or bad weather.

Different homes

Hermit crabs make their homes in an empty seashell.

Squirrels make warm homes called dreys from twigs and leaves.

Clownfish live among the stinging tentacles of sea anemones.

Tortoises have mobile homes – their hard shells protect them.

Marmosets make a different home every night in the treetops.

Rabbit warren
Wild rabbits live together in a warren – a system of underground tunnels and rooms.

When baby rabbits grow up, they also live in the warren.

Entrance is dug into the earth or among tree roots.

Baby rabbits live in nests called stops.

Underground rooms called burrows

Termite nest
Termites build amazing nests housing up to five million termites.

Network of cells and tunnels made from dried mud

Some nests are 40 ft (12 m) tall!

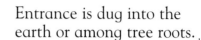

Did you know?
A female polar bear and her cubs sleep all winter in a warm den under the snow.

Find out more Animal families 15 Eggs and nests 51

World of Nature

Animals

There are more than ten million different species of animals in the world. Scientists have divided them into two main groups.

Mammals, such as humans, live mainly on land. Only a few live in the sea.

Vertebrates

Fish live in the world's rivers, lakes, and oceans. They take in oxygen through their gills.

Invertebrates

Starfish and sea urchins belong to a group of animals with spiny skins.

Octopuses and squid have soft bodies. They are related to mollusks, but do not have a shell.

Amphibians, such as frogs and toads, live both on land and in water.

Reptiles, such as snakes, lay eggs on land and have dry, scaly skins.

Mollusks, such as snails, have hard shells to protect them from enemies and sun.

Insects, such as beetles, have a hard outer skeleton.

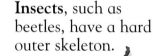

Birds are animals with beaks, feathers, and wings. Most of them can fly.

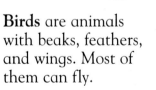

Crustaceans, such as crabs, shed their shells when they grow too big for them. A new shell grows underneath.

Vertebrates

Vertebrates are animals with backbones. They are split into five main groups.

Invertebrates

Invertebrates are animals with no backbones. Many have hard shells or a tough outer skeleton to protect them.

Find out more ➤ Living things 91   Skeletons 128

17

World of Nature

Animals in danger

Large copper butterflies are very nearly extinct because their marshy habitat is being destroyed.

All over the world, wild animals are in danger. Some are killed for their skins, others live in areas called habitats that are being destroyed. These animals need our protection.

Protecting animals

Habitat destruction
Wild animals can die out due to lack of food and shelter if their habitat is destroyed.

Orangutans' rain forest habitats are being destroyed as trees are cut down to make way for farms.

Large nature reserves give animals like elephants the space they need to live.

Hunting
Wild cats, snakes, and crocodiles are hunted for their beautiful skins, as well as other parts of their bodies.

Tigers are in danger of extinction because they are killed for their claws and teeth, used in Chinese medicines.

Zoos help rare animals like eagles breed. The young can then be released into the wild.

Snakes are killed by the thousands to make snakeskin bags and shoes.

Laws ban rare animals such as tortoises from being sold as pets.

Did you know?
There are fewer than 200 pandas left in China's forests.

Pollution
Factory waste and farm chemicals can pollute the land, air, and water, poisoning many wild animals.

Seals can die from diseases caught from the polluted water in which they live.

Laws ban goods made from the skins of certain animals, like crocodiles.

Find out more   Asia 24   Conservation 43

Continents of the World

Antarctica

Antarctica is a vast, ice-covered continent near the south pole. No one lives here permanently. It is the coldest and windiest place on Earth.

Did you know?
- Antarctica is bigger than Europe and the US put together.
- Antarctica is actually a desert! It gets no rain all year round.

Research station

Antarctic summer
In some places, the ice melts in summer. But the ground remains frozen.

QUEEN
MAUD
LAND

ANTARCTIC PENINSULA

ELLSWORTH
MOUNTAINS

ENDERBY LAND

TRANSANTARCTIC MOUNTAINS

◆ South Pole

MARIE BYRD
LAND

A N T A R C T I C A

ROSS ICE
SHELF

WILKES LAND

Iceberg
Icebergs are huge chunks of ice that break off from the land and float in the ocean.

Scientists
Scientists from around the world visit Antarctica to study the land and its wildlife.

South pole
The south pole is the most southerly point on the Earth.

Explorers at south pole

Minerals
Below the ice and rock lie coal, copper, gold, and other valuable materials.

Tourism
Tourists admire Antarctica's scenery from large cruise ships.

Wildlife
Some animals and a few simple plants have adapted to life here. The animals hunt for food in the ocean.

Albatross

Penguins

Moss

Leopard seal

Find out more Explorers 61   Polar lands 112

Continents of the World

Asia

Eastern Asia
Eastern Asia is a vast area that has many great rivers, dry deserts, windy highlands, and flat, grassy plains.

Rafflesia plant
This flower is the largest in the world.

Mount Fuji
Mount Fuji is Japan's highest and most beautiful mountain.

Yangtze River
The Yangtze River in China is the third longest river in the world.

Tibet
Tibet is so high above sea level that it is known as the roof of the world.

Gobi Desert
The rocky Gobi Desert is very hot in summer, but cold and windy in winter.

Mangrove swamps
Mangrove trees grow along the coasts of the region's islands.

Map labels:
ULAN BATOR
MONGOLIA
GOBI DESERT
TAKLA MAKAN DESERT
CHINA
Yellow River
BEIJING
NORTH KOREA
PYONGYANG
SEOUL
SOUTH KOREA
JAPAN
TOKYO
Mount Fuji
TIBET
Yangtze River
GUANGXI ZHUANG
TAIPEI
TAIWAN
BURMA
HANOI
HONG KONG
MACAO
Hainan
VIENTIANE
VIETNAM
LAOS
THAILAND
RANGOON
Luzon
MANILA
BANGKOK
CAMBODIA
PHNOM PENH
PHILIPPINES
Mindanao
BRUNEI
MALAYSIA
KUALA LUMPUR
BANDAR SERI BEGAWAN
SINGAPORE
Sumatra
Borneo
Moluccas
Celebes
Irian Jaya
JAKARTA
Java
INDONESIA
N

Thailand's coastline
Parts of the Thai coastline have strange rocky towers and steep cliff faces.

Did you know?
- There are more volcanoes in eastern Asia than anywhere else in the world.
- The country of Indonesia is made up of more than 13,000 islands.

Rain forest
Thick tropical rain forest grows on the hillsides of many of the islands.

Panda
Pandas live in the mountains of China. They feed on bamboo leaves.

Find out more Mammals of the world 95 Rain forests 114

Continents of the World

Asia: culture

Eastern Asia
Many people in eastern Asia live on quiet farms. Others work in high-tech factories in busy cities.

Population
One-fifth of the world's population lives in China.

Factory workers

Industry, Japan
Japan is a world leader in producing televisions and other electrical and high-technology goods.

Television production line

Electronic circuit board

Culture
Buddhism is a very important religion in much of Southeast Asia.

Temple

Shadow puppets have been popular entertainment in Indonesia for hundreds of years.

Lacquered goods, such as this plate, are made in Thailand.

Kimonos are traditional Japanese dress. These gowns are made of silk.

Village life
Many Asian people live in small, country villages. They farm the land in traditional ways.

Rubber trees
In Malaysia, the sap from rubber trees is collected and turned into rubber.

Food and drink
Rice, tea, and wheat are grown in the region. Fresh fish is a very important food.

Jasmine tea

Rice

Raw fish dish

Korean dish

Folk music is very popular. The nomads of Mongolia sing to the music of a fiddle.

Fiddle

Find out more ▶ Factories 62   Theater 139

Asia

Northern Asia

Northern Asia encompasses frozen lands in the north and rolling grasslands and barren deserts in the south.

Did you know?
- The Caspian Sea is the largest lake in the world. It is four times the size of Portugal.
- Lake Baikal is the oldest and deepest lake on Earth.

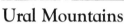

Siberia
In the north of Asia, there is a vast, snow-covered area called Siberia.

Iris
The Siberian iris flowers in the summer months.

Ural Mountains
These mountains have been worn down by the weather over hundreds of years.

Tundra
Much of Siberia is a frozen, treelesss plain called the tundra.

N

BELARUS
MINSK

UKRAINE
KIEV
• MOSCOW

BLACK SEA

Volga River

URAL MOUNTAINS

R U S S I A N
F E D E R A T I O N

SIBERIA

Lena River

Kolyma River

KAMCHATKA

GEORGIA

ARMENIA

AZERBAIJAN

CASPIAN SEA

K A Z A K H S T A N

Ob' River

Yenisey River

STANOVOY RANGE

Capital cities
1 TBILISI
2 YEREVAN
3 BAKU
4 ASHGABAT
5 DUSHANBE
6 TASHKENT
7 BISHKEK
8 ALMATY

TURKMENISTAN

UZBEKISTAN

ARAL SEA

Lake Balkhash

TAJIKISTAN

KYRGYSTAN

Lake Baikal

Husky dogs
In Siberia, people use huskies to pull sleds across the snow.

Volga River
The Volga River flows over 2,000 miles (3,500 km) into the Caspian Sea.

Aral Sea
This large saltwater lake lies in dry desert land.

Lake Baikal
Lake Baikal is fed by more than 300 rivers and is home to many rare animals.

Find out more Polar animals 111 Polar lands 112

Polar animals 111   Polar lands 112

Asia: culture

Did you know?

In winter, Siberian children stand under sun lamps. It's meant to keep them healthy.

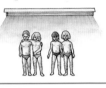

Northern Asia

The Russian Federation is the biggest country in the world, with many different peoples and cultures.

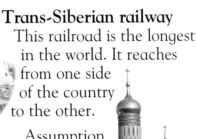

Trans-Siberian railway
This railroad is the longest in the world. It reaches from one side of the country to the other.

Regional foods

Borscht is a famous soup made from beetroot. It comes from the Ukraine.

Caviar, the eggs of the sturgeon fish, is a very expensive delicacy.

Kremlin, Moscow

The Kremlin was once home to the Russian Czars. It now houses the government.

Grand Kremlin Palace

Archangel Cathedral

Assumption Cathedral

Bread is an important part of the Russian diet.

Industry

Heavy industries, such as iron and steel making, have led to problems with air pollution in the region.

Mining is very important. Coal, gold, and diamonds are all mined here.

Sulfur

Coal

Draniki is the national dish of Belarus. It is made from grated potatoes.

Craftwork

Fur hat

Silk scarf

Russian dolls

Balalaika

Russian peoples

Different peoples, such as the Russian Cossacks and the Kyrgyz nomads, all have different customs.

Russian Cossacks

Kyrgyz nomads

Find out more Rocks and minerals 120 Transportation 142

Continents of the World

Asia

Western and Southern Asia
Some of the world's hottest deserts and highest mountains lie in this part of the Asian continent.

Hot pools
These amazing hot pools in Turkey are made of minerals.

Desert
Sandy desert covers most of Saudi Arabia.

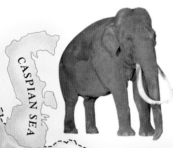

Indian elephant
Elephants live in the forests of India.

Mount Everest
Mount Everest, in the Himalayas, is the highest mountain in the world.

Capital cities
1 NICOSIA
2 BEIRUT
3 JERUSALEM
4 MANAMA
5 DOHA
6 ABU DHABI
7 MUSCAT

BLACK SEA

•ANKARA

CYPRUS 1•

TURKEY

CASPIAN SEA

LEBANON
2• •SYRIA
ISRAEL •DAMASCUS
3• IRAQ
•AMMAN •BAGHDAD
JORDAN

•TEHRAN

IRAN

AFGHANISTAN
•KABUL

KASHMIR

PAKISTAN
•ISLAMABAD

Indus River

Mount Everest

KUWAIT
KUWAIT CITY•

SAUDI
ARABIA
•RIYADH •

BAHRAIN
4•
QATAR
5•

6•
UNITED
ARAB
EMIRATES 7•

NEW DELHI•

NEPAL
KATHMANDU•

THIMPHU•
•BHUTAN

Ganges River

BANGLADESH
•DACCA

RED SEA

EMPTY
QUARTER

N

INDIA

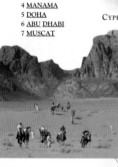

Wadi
Desert rivers often dry up, leaving rocky riverbeds called wadis.

SAN'A• YEMEN OMAN

Red Sea
The Red Sea divides northern Africa from western Asia.

Ganges River
This river carries water to a large part of India and Bangladesh.

Kashmir
Kashmir is a land of lakes and mountains.

SRI LANKA
•COLOMBO

Sri Lanka
The island of Sri Lanka is fringed with white, sandy beaches.

Continents of the World

Asia: culture

Products

Jute is grown in Bangladesh to make sacking and rope.

Oranges and other citrus fruits are grown in Israel.

Tea is grown on large plantations in India and Sri Lanka.

Oil is drilled in the desert countries in the west.

Bollywood, Bombay
This is the center of India's film industry.

Western and Southern Asia
Most people here still live in small villages, but many are moving to the cities for work.

Taj Mahal, Agra
This marble tomb in India was built as a memorial to the wife of an emperor. It is over 350 years old.

Riyadh

The city of Riyadh in Saudi Arabia was built with money from oil. All its buildings are new.

Delicate design

White marble walls

Beautiful towers on both sides

Food
Spices and fruit are used to flavor many dishes.

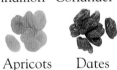

Cinnamon   Coriander   Turmeric

Apricots   Dates   Garlic

Nomads
Nomads still live in parts of Asia, moving from place to place.

Craftwork
The craftwork in this part of Asia is brightly colored and highly decorated.

Child's hat

Indian dress

Sitar

Turkish rug

Did you know?
In Bhutan, archery competitors jump in front of the targets to distract each other!

Australasia

Australia and Papua New Guinea

From mountains and rain forests to deserts and coral reefs, Australasia has a varied landscape and unique wildlife.

Did you know?
- Australia has many animals that live nowhere else in the world.
- The Great Barrier Reef is the largest living structure on Earth.

Blue Mountains
The Blue Mountains run down the eastern coast of Australia.

Rain forest
Tropical rain forest covers over two-thirds of Papua New Guinea.

Desert rocks
These strange desert rocks in western Australia are called the Pinnacles.

Great Barrier Reef
The Great Barrier Reef is a long line of reefs and islands. It is made of living coral.

N

PAPUA NEW GUINEA

• PORT MORESBY

ARNHEM LAND

NORTHERN TERRITORY

GREAT SANDY DESERT

A U S T R A L I A

MACDONNELL RANGES

GIBSON DESERT

Uluru (Ayers Rock)

WESTERN AUSTRALIA

GREAT VICTORIA DESERT

SOUTH AUSTRALIA

QUEENSLAND

GREAT DIVIDING RANGE

GREAT BARRIER REEF

Darling River

NEW SOUTH WALES

BLUE MOUNTAINS

Murray River

CANBERRA

VICTORIA

AUSTRALIAN CAPITAL TERRITORY

TASMANIA

Koala bear
Koalas live in eucalyptus woods in eastern Australia, feeding on the leaves of the trees.

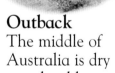

Outback
The middle of Australia is dry grassland known as the outback.

Tasmanian devil
This fierce animal has sharp teeth and a nasty snarl. It lives only in Tasmania.

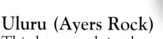

Uluru (Ayers Rock)
This huge rock in the desert is a sacred place for Aboriginals, the first people of Australia.

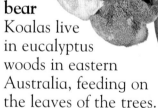

Tasmania
Tasmania is a small island that lies south of Australia.

Find out more Birds of the world 31   Seas and oceans 124

Continents of the World

Australasia

New Zealand and Pacific Islands

Hot springs, volcanoes, and white, sandy beaches are just some of the features of New Zealand and the Pacific islands.

Did you know?
- New Zealand's most beautiful areas are protected as national parks.
- There are about 30,000 islands in the Pacific Ocean.

PACIFIC ISLANDS

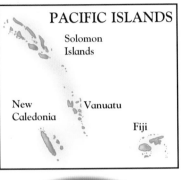

Solomon Islands

New Caledonia

Vanuatu

Fiji

Fiji
Fiji is made up of 322 islands. Much of the land is covered with forest and surrounded by coral reefs.

N

NORTH ISLAND

Lake Taupo

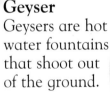

Kiwi
Kiwi birds cannot fly. They live in New Zealand.

Mud pools
Heat from inside the Earth makes hot mud pools in New Zealand.

Mount Cook
Mount Cook is the highest mountain in New Zealand.

Tropical island
The Pacific islands have long, sandy beaches and sparkling blue seas.

• WELLINGTON

SOUTH ISLAND

N E W   Z E A L A N D

SOUTHERN ALPS

Mount Cook ▲

Lake Wakatipu

Lake Te Anau

Stewart Island

Geyser
Geysers are hot water fountains that shoot out of the ground.

Kakapo
This New Zealand parrot is very rare. It is too heavy to fly.

Fjord
New Zealand's coastline has deep inlets called fjords.

Sheep
The wet climate provides good grazing for sheep.

Volcano
There are many active volcanoes in New Zealand.

Lake
Beautiful freshwater lakes fill the craters in the mountains.

Find out more Birds of the world 31   Seas and oceans 124

Continents of the World

Australasia: culture

The people of Australasia have different lifestyles. Some still lead a traditional life, far from the nearest town. Others live busy lives in modern, crowded cities.

Sports
Rugby is a very popular sport in Fiji.

Sydney Opera House
This modern opera house overlooks Sydney Harbour. Most cities in Australia are on the coast.

Tribes
There are more than 1,000 different tribes in Papua New Guinea.

The arched roofs look like the sails of yachts.

White-tiled roofs

Sydney Harbour

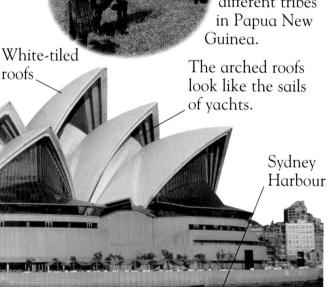

Farming

Wool from sheep farms is sold all over the world.

Orange

Tamarillo

Peach

Fruit farming suits New Zealand's warm, wet climate.

Mining
Mining is important. Gold, gemstones, coal, iron, and copper are all mined in Australia.

Gold

Opal

Tourism
The stunning scenery and relaxing lifestyle attract many tourists.

Did you know?
Some Australian farms are so large, farmers use planes to get across them.

Aboriginal and Maori people

Aboriginal people settled in Australia more than 50,000 years ago.

Aboriginal bark painting

Maori people came to New Zealand over 1,000 years ago.

Maori carving

Find out more Farm animals 63   Painting 107

Bicycles

Bikes are a popular transportation choice because they are cheap, easy to repair, and keep us healthy. Add an engine, and you have a motorcycle.

Bicycle
Bikes are machines. They are moved by cyclists pushing the pedals around with their feet.

Tires are filled with air, which helps cushion bumps.

Saddle

Handlebars are used to steer the bike.

Frame

Spokes

Pedals

Brakes stop the bike.

Gears give cyclists more power.

Chain links pedals to back wheel

Pannier
Panniers can be attached to a bike to carry things.

Riding a bicycle
Learning to ride a bike is a tricky skill. It takes a good sense of balance.

Types of bicycles

Road bikes are light but strong for use on bumpy roads.

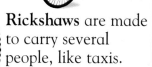

Rickshaws are made to carry several people, like taxis.

Unicycles are often seen in circuses. Balancing on one wheel is difficult!

Tripletandems are for three riders. They have three seats and three sets of pedals!

Cantilevers are the most modern racing bikes. They have streamlined frames.

Motorcycles
Motorcycles are more complicated machines than bikes. Powerful engines move them.

Engine   Fuel tank

Scooters have small engines. They are popular for traveling around town.

Motocross bikes are used for racing across rough country.

World of Nature

Birds

Birds come in all shapes and sizes and are the only animals with feathers. They have a beak but no teeth, and their babies hatch out of eggs.

Did you know?
The ostrich is too heavy to fly, but it can run fast!

Ears are hidden under feathers.

The shape of a bird's beak tells you what it eats.

A bird has wings instead of arms.

Eyes are sharp to spot food.

Tail is used for balance.

Robin
Like most birds, this robin has a light, streamlined body, which helps it fly.

Leg

Claws grip branches and grab food.

Beaks and food

Hummingbirds suck nectar with their long beaks.

Parrots crack open hard nuts with their beaks.

Eagles kill small animals with their sharp beaks.

Flamingos scoop up algae and tiny fish.

Finches peck at seeds and nuts.

Feathers
Long tail and wing feathers are used for flight and balance. While soft, downy chest feathers keep a bird warm.

Chest feathers

Wing feathers

Flying
A bird stays up in the air by flapping its strong wings. Some birds can glide on the wind.

Pigeon

The feathers close up and push down against the air.

As the wings rise, the feathers spread apart.

Find out more ➤ Birds of the world 31   Eggs and nests 51

World of Nature

Birds of the world

There are more than 8,500 different birds, and they live in every part of the world. Each bird's body and feeding habits have evolved to suit where it lives.

Did you know?
The rhinoceros hornbill has a box on its beak that makes its call so loud it can be heard over 1 mile (2 km) away.

Barn owl
The barn owl lives in northern Europe, feeding on small mammals.

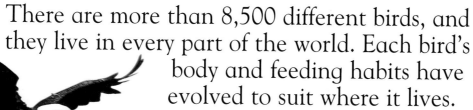

Bald eagle
The bald eagle, found in North America, swoops down to grab its prey.

Shelduck
The shelduck feeds on small shellfish. It is found on river estuaries in Southeast Asia.

Toucan
Toucans live in the hot, steamy rain forests of South America, eating tropical fruit.

NORTH AMERICA
ARCTIC OCEAN
EUROPE
ASIA
PACIFIC OCEAN
ATLANTIC OCEAN
AFRICA
SOUTH AMERICA
INDIAN OCEAN
AUSTRALASIA
ANTARCTICA

Kiwi
Kiwis can't fly. They live only in New Zealand.

Scarlet macaw
Macaws live on the edge of South American rain forests. They eat fruit, nuts, and seeds.

Sunbirds
Native to Africa, scarlet-chested sunbirds eat insects and nectar.

Emperor penguin
Penguins live in icy cold Antarctica. They can't fly, but are excellent swimmers.

Flamingo
Many flamingos live by hot lakes in Africa. They feed on tiny shrimps and algae.

Cockatoo
Living on the Australian grasslands, cockatoos feed on seeds and leaves.

Find out more Birds 30 Eggs and nests 51

Life Today

Books

The words and pictures inside books provide readers with information, ideas, and fun.

Library
Public libraries are places where people can read and borrow many different kinds of books.

Novelty books
Novelty books have pop-ups, flaps, and stickers to make reading fun.

sheep   goose

Nonfiction
Nonfiction books are about the real world. They contain facts, pictures, and photographs.

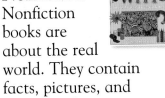

Book shelves   Study desk

Fiction
Fiction books contain made-up stories. Children's fiction often has pictures.

Shortcut

CD-Roms
CD-Roms are information discs read by computers. They have pictures, words, and sounds.

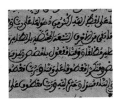

Writing
To write, people use a collection of letters and symbols called an alphabet.

The **Chinese** use symbols called characters.

Arabic words read from right to left.

"But who is to give the prizes?" quite a chorus of voices asked.
"Why, *she*, of course," said the Dodo, pointing to Alice with one finger; and the whole party at once crowded round her, calling out in a confused way, "Prizes! Prizes!"
Alice had no idea what to do, and in despair she put her hand into her pocket, and pulled out a box of comfits, (luckily the salt water had not got into it,) and handed them round as prizes. There was exactly one a-piece, all round.

The **Roman alphabet** is used around the world.

Braille books
Braille books use a special alphabet of raised dots that blind people "read" with their fingers.

Find out more Ancient Greece 14   Human body: senses 81

Science and Technology

Bridges and tunnels

Types of bridges

Brenner Bridge
Beam bridges are supported by strong columns called piers.

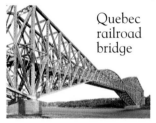

Quebec railroad bridge

Cantilever bridges balance the deck on strong supports.

Tyne Bridge
Arch bridges push their weight into the banks of a river.

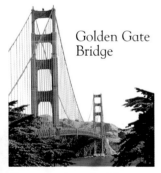

Golden Gate Bridge

Suspension bridges hang from cables held up by towers.

Everywhere we go there are obstacles to cross. Bridges and tunnels make it easy to travel over or under rivers, across valleys, and through mountains.

Forth Rail Bridge, Scotland
The deck of this cantilever bridge is made of two pieces, built out from the banks.

Support tower

Deck of bridge

Steel girders

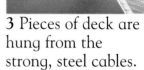

Building a suspension bridge

1 Huge cranes build tall columns, called piers, on each side of a river.

2 The towers are built. These are the strongest part of the bridge.

3 Pieces of deck are hung from the strong, steel cables.

Tunnel
Tunnels burrow under barriers such as mountains, seas, and crowded city streets.

Road tunnel through a mountain

Train coming out of a tunnel under the sea

Huge drilling machines bore tunnels through obstacles.

Find out more → Building machines 34 ⬥ Europe: culture 56

Science and Technology

Building machines

In the past, many great buildings were built by hand and took years to complete. Today's powerful machines make building work much quicker and easier.

Bulldozer
A bulldozer clears and flattens the ground, ready for building.

Big steel bucket pushes earth aside

Exhaust pipe

Driver's cab

Crawler tracks can move over rough ground.

Handheld machines
Not all machines on building sites are huge trucks. Some are much smaller machines.

Pneumatic drill

Cement mixer

Wheelbarrow

Demolition ball
Demolition balls smash down old buildings so that new ones can be built in their place.

Building site
Many machines are used on building sites. They are busy and dangerous places to work.

Crane

Concrete mixer

Types of building machines

Concrete mixers bring ready-mixed concrete to a site.

Excavators dig out trenches, where pipes and foundations will be laid.

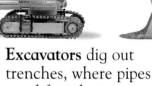

Dump trucks bring all the building materials to a site.

Backhoe loaders dig trenches and then remove the rubble.

Truck loader cranes lift heavy loads to the top of a building.

Science and Technology

Buildings

Every building has a purpose – whether it's for leisure, worship, or work. But each one is different – built from a mix of materials in a variety of styles.

Did you know?
Tall skyscrapers are built to sway slightly in strong winds.

Place of worship
St. Basil's Cathedral in Russia was built to celebrate a victory in war. Today it is used as a museum.

Walls are built of brick.

Large central tower

Dome

Turret

Brick mosaic
Colored bricks have been used to make flower mosaics.

Uses of buildings

Offices are built in town and city centers, where many people go to work.

Chrysler Building

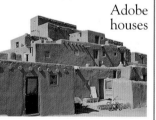

Sydney Opera House

Theater and opera houses are buildings with large seating halls inside.

Adobe houses

Houses are different around the world, and are built of a variety of materials.

Beachy Head Lighthouse

Lighthouses are built to warn ships of rocky coasts and sandbanks.

Building materials
Builders use materials that are strong, weatherproof, and easy to find.

Tiles on roofs keep out rain. They can be made of clay.

Wooden beams can hold up floors and ceilings.

Bricks can be stuck together in rows to build walls.

Thatch is made of reeds or straw. It makes a waterproof roof.

Find out more Homes and houses 78 Towns and cities 140

World of Nature

Butterflies and moths

With their colorful wings, butterflies are the most beautiful insects. Moths are less colorful because most of them fly at night.

A butterfly's mouth, called a proboscis, is like a long, curly straw.

Scaly wings

Butterflies smell with their antennae.

Head

Defense
Eyespots on the wings of this butterfly frighten enemies away.

Banana eater

This butterfly camouflages itself by pretending to be a leaf.

Leaf butterfly

Thorax Abdomen

Swallowtail butterfly
Butterflies and moths are insects. Like this swallowtail, they all have three body parts, six legs, and four large wings.

Growing up

1 Butterfly eggs hatch out into caterpillars.

2 A caterpillar grows so fast it must keep shedding its skin.

3 The fully grown caterpillar slowly makes a hard case called a chrysalis.

4 About four weeks later, a butterfly crawls out and dries its wings.

Citrus swallowtail

Moth facts

Thick, furry body

Large, feathery antennae

Wings spread out when resting

Butterfly facts

Slender body

Smooth antennae with clublike ends

Wings folded when resting

Did you know?
This African moth has a proboscis three times as long as its body to suck nectar from exotic flowers.

Find out more Insects 86   Spiders and mini-beasts 134

Science and Technology

Cars

Cars come in all shapes and sizes and are used by all sorts of people. The job a car does determines its looks, its performance, and its price!

Family car
Engineers use computers to create the design for a car, such as this family station wagon.

Baby car seat
Babies sit in small seats with straps to keep them safe.

Airbag
Airbags fill up with air to protect people in a crash.

Large luggage space

Five comfortable passenger seats

Streamlined shape

Small engine cuts down fuel consumption

Turn signals warn other drivers when the car is going to turn.

Mirror
Car mirrors help drivers see the road behind them.

|Wheel

Tire
Different cars use different kinds of tires.

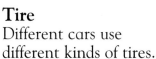

Road tire   Race car tire

Did you know?
The world's longest car has 26 wheels and a tiny swimming pool on board!

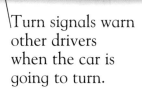

Types of cars

Classic cars are old, stylish cars that have survived from the early years of car design.

Police cars are fitted with radios, sirens, and other special equipment.

Customized cars have been chopped up, added to, and painted to make them look unusual.

All-terrain vehicles have powerful engines. Big wheels keep a grip on muddy tracks.

Battery-run car
This car is for a disabled driver. It's environmentally friendly because it runs on a battery, not fuel.

Race cars have room only for the driver. They are low, streamlined, and fast.

Find out more Factories 62   Trucks 144

Life in the Past

Castles

Castles were once the homes of kings and lords. These strong buildings protected them from their enemies.

Types of castles

Saumur castle lies on the banks of the Loire River in France. It has tall, pointed towers.

Flag
The flag carried the lord's coat of arms.

Drawbridge
Pulling up the drawbridge cut the castle off from enemies.

Spanish castle
This castle has two sets of thick stone walls. It was built in 1475 and became a luxury palace.

El Real de Manzanares

Turrets

Arrow loop
Archers fired arrows through slits in the walls.

Battlements

Portcullis
A metal grille protected the wooden gates.

Caerphilly castle is the largest castle in Wales. It was built between 1268–1271.

Krak des Chevaliers was a huge Crusader fortress. It could house over 2,000 soldiers.

Neuschwanstein looks like a fairy-tale castle. It was built in Germany in the 1800s.

Laying siege
In a siege, an enemy army surrounded a castle and attacked it with powerful weapons.

Giant catapults hurled rocks and stones at the castle walls.

George du Dades castle in Morocco has very high walls. It was hard to attack.

Crossbows
fired arrows at soldiers on the castle battlements.

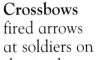

Cannons began to be used in about 1350.

Archers were specially trained to fire crossbows.

Find out more ▶ Buildings 35   Europe: culture 58

World of Nature

Climates

Every part of the world has its own climate, a pattern of weather that is roughly the same every year and affects the plants that grow there.

Cold forest spruce Scotland

Desert climate
Namibia
A desert climate is very dry. Most deserts have burning hot days and freezing cold nights.

Desert cactus

Cold forest climate
This has long, snowy winters, and short, cool summers.

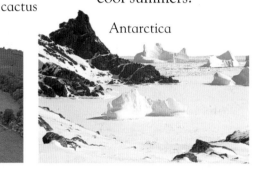
Antarctica

Tropical climate
Malaysia
This climate is hot all year round. There is heavy rain every day for many months of the year.

Rain forest leaf

Temperate climate
England
This climate has warm summers and cool winters. It rains most months of the year.

Temperate leaf

Polar climate
Polar climates are cold and icy all year round. They are also very dry.

Polar lichen

What affects the climate

The land
The higher you climb, the colder it gets. High places, such as mountains, have cold climates.

The sun
The sun is hotter near the equator and cooler at the poles. A place is hot or cold depending on where it lies.

The sea
Places near the sea have milder climates than places inland. The summers are cool, the winters are mild.

Science and Technology

Color

A world without color would be a dull place. The beautiful colors around us are actually different kinds of light.

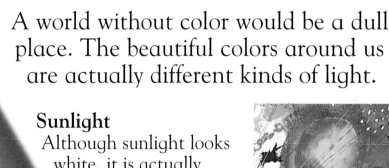

Sunlight

Although sunlight looks white, it is actually made up of many different colors. You can see these colors in a rainbow.

_____ Red

_____ Orange

_____ Yellow

_____ Green

_____ Blue

_____ Indigo

_____ Violet

Seeing in color

When rays of light hit this painting, some of the colors in the light are soaked up. Others bounce back into our eyes.

Primary colors

The primary colors are red, blue, and yellow. By mixing these, any other color can be made.

Paint

Paint was once made from natural sources.

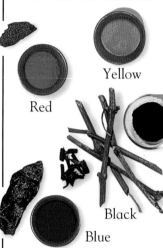

Red

Yellow

Black

Blue

Rocks or plants were crushed to make a colored powder. This was mixed with oil.

Today, most of the paints we use have been made from chemicals.

Life without color

Colors affect our feelings about things. Which of these meals would you rather eat?

Color in nature

Colors help animals communicate. This frog's bright colors warn that it is poisonous.

Peacocks attract mates with their colorful feathers.

Did you know?

Chameleons change color when they feel angry, frightened, or too hot or cold.

Find out more Light 90 Painting 107

Science and Technology

Communications

Sign language
Some deaf people use a system of hand signals to communicate.

Talking, writing, and reading are all ways in which people share their thoughts and ideas. This is known as communication.

Did you know?
Native Americans used smoke signals to communicate quickly across long distances.

Talking
When people talk they use their voices, facial expressions, and hands to help say what they mean.

We look at each other when we talk.

Telephone
Mobile phones turn voices into radio waves, which are sent around the world by satellites.

One-way communication

Internet
The Internet is a world-wide computer system that people use to exchange messages.

Televisions pick up radio waves and change them into sounds and pictures.

Videophone
This phone has a TV picture of the person at the other end.

Radios pick up sound waves that travel invisibly through the air.

Writing
The earliest writing was carved on stone. Now we can print words quickly and easily.

Letters are delivered around the world by planes, trains, vans, and people.

Magazines and newspapers are a popular way of spreading information.

Fax machines use phone lines to send documents to other fax machines.

Find out more ▷ Books 32   Television 138

Science and Technology

Computers

Computers don't just sit on desks. They are the superfast electronic brains behind many of the machines we use in everyday life.

Calculator

A calculator is a small computer that can figure out complicated arithmetic fast.

Virtual reality

With virtual reality machines you can imagine you are at the controls of a supersonic jet or spacecraft.

Games

Computer games are just for fun!

Robot

Robots do many different jobs in factories. In car factories, computers "tell" robots how to assemble a car.

Headset has a mini-TV screen

As you move your head, different images appear on the TV screen.

Controls

Motors rock the machine to make the "journey" more realistic.

Flight simulator

Pilots train in simulators on the ground. Computers make it look as if they are flying in the air.

Movies

In many movies, computers create amazing special effects.

Design

Designers use computers to create pictures of their ideas, such as a new car.

Personal computer

These computers can be used in many ways, from playing games to doing homework.

Screen

Disk drive

Keyboard

Chips are the "brain" of a computer.

A hard disk stores information inside the computer.

A laptop is a personal computer that you can carry around.

Did you know?

The first computer was so big it filled up a whole room!

Find out more Inventions 88 Space travel 133

Conservation

Conservation means looking after the Earth's resources – plants, animals, air, water, and land. It's a world problem, but one that begins at home.

Clean air
Cars use fuel and pump dirty exhaust fumes into the air.

Walking to school instead of going by car helps keep the air clean.

Cycling is a clean form of transportation. It does not pollute the air.

Recycling
Recycling means collecting old materials and using them to make new materials.

1 Used glass bottles are collected at home.

2 Used glass is put into special collection bins.

3 Glass is taken to a recycling factory.

Each bin is for different materials.

Glass is melted down to make new products.

Recycled glass bottles

Clean water
Garbage and poisons pollute water. This can be dangerous.

People, plants, and animals need clean water to live.

Dirty, polluted water causes sickness and infection.

Clean Earth
Chemicals and garbage pollute the land. They stay in the soil for many years.

Picking up litter keeps the environment clean.

Organic crops are grown without chemicals – keeping the soil clean.

Energy
Burning fuels to make electricity uses up resources.

Recycled glass bulb

Switching off lights saves energy.

Modern wind machines produce electricity without burning fuels.

Find out more   Energy 54   Materials 97

Dance

Life Today

Types of dance

Thai dances are graceful. They were first performed in temples.

Rock and roll dance began in America in the 1950s.

Native American dances all have special meanings.

Country-and-western dance is popular and lots of fun.

Folk dances are the old, traditional dances of a country.

Dancing is moving your body to music. People dance alone, with a partner, or in groups. There are dancing styles around the world.

Spanish flamenco
Flamenco dancing comes from Spain. The dancers stamp and whirl to the music of a guitar.

Long, colorful dresses

Dancers toss their heads.

Flowers are worn in hair.

Castanets are cliked in a rhythm.

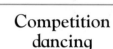

Competition dancing

Ballroom dancers are judged on their steps, style, and grace.

Disco dancers are judged on their energy and original movements.

Ballet
Ballet tells stories through dance. It has five basic body positions that combine into many movements.

First   Second   Third   Fourth   Fifth

Ballet dancers are strong and fit. They train for many years.

Find out more

 Europe: culture 60   Music 100

World of Nature

Desert animals

With burning days, freezing nights, and no water, a desert is one of the harshest habitats on Earth. Even so, some animals manage to survive here.

Desert shelter
Like many desert animals, fennec foxes shelter from the sun in underground burrows.

Desert survival

Harris's hawks build their nests in the prickly branches of cacti.

Bactrian camel
Camels have adapted well to desert life. They can go without water for months.

Thick fur protects the camel from the burning sun.

Humps store fat for when food is scarce.

Nostrils can close to keep out sand.

Dwarf hamsters have thick fur to help them survive freezing desert nights.

Darkling wing beetles have white wings to reflect heat, keeping the insects cool.

Wide feet prevent sinking in soft sand.

Stomach stores water.

Desert reptiles

Lizard

Many reptiles live in the desert. Their scaly skin stops them from drying out.

Tadpole shrimps can survive under the sand for 10 years, waiting for rain to fall.

Did you know?
Male sandgrouse soak up water in their breast feathers and then fly back to their chicks, who drink it all up!

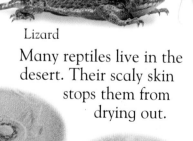

Sand viper

To escape from the sun, the sand viper buries itself in sand.

Scorpions hunt only in the cool of the night. They kill their prey with a deadly sting.

World of Nature

Deserts

Desert plants

Kokerboom trees can survive for several years without water.

Barrel cacti store water inside their thick, waxy spines and stems.

Hedgehog cacti grow in rocky deserts and flower when it rains.

Century plants bloom once every 20 to 50 years.

Whisker cactus flowers open at night because most insects feed when it's cool.

Deserts are the driest places on Earth. Instead of soil, the land is covered with bare rock, gravel, or sand, so very few plants can grow.

Rocky desert
Hot days, freezing nights, and strong winds make desert rocks splinter and crack.

Did you know?
The San people of Africa find tiny wells in the desert. They suck up the water through hollow sticks.

Sandy desert
Strong desert winds blow sand into ever-changing hills called sand dunes.

Sand dunes can be as tall as a 60-story skyscraper.

An oasis is a place where water flows out of the ground.

Palms and other plants can grow here.

Desert life
People who live in the desert move around, looking for water and grazing land for their animals. They are called nomads.

Bedouin nomads

Saluki dogs are used for hunting.

Arabian horses are used for transportation.

Many nomads use cloth tents to shelter from the burning sun.

Find out more Desert animals 45 South America 130

Dinosaur types

Did you know?

The longest dinosaur was *Seismosaurus*. At 131 ft (40 m) it was longer than many modern planes.

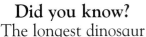

Dinosaurs ruled the Earth for 165 million years. There were more than 300 different kinds, but they didn't all live at the same time!

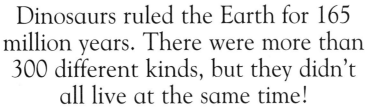

Edmontonia
Edmontonia had spiky body armor. This made it hard to attack.

Ducklike beak

Head shapes

Oviraptor ate eggs, cracking the shells with its pointed beak.

Corythosaurus
Corythosaurus was a duck-billed dinosaur. It lived in the Cretaceous period, and fed on leaves.

Long tail for balance

Strong back legs to run from danger

Front legs pulled down branches.

Bony crest

Troodon
Troodon used its huge, curved claws to catch its prey.

Psittacosaurus
Psittacosaurus used its horny beak to strip leaves from trees.

Stegocerous used its strong, bony skull to head-butt its enemies.

Compsognathus had a long neck, narrow jaws, and sharp teeth.

Euoplocephalus
Leathery skin and spikes protected *Euoplocephalus* from its enemies.

Deinonychus
Deinonychus was a fast and deadly hunter, with strong teeth and sharp claws.

Iguanodon
Iguanodon was a large plant eater with a sharp beak.

Triceratops had three horns and a frill to protect its neck.

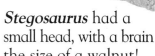

Stegosaurus had a small head, with a brain the size of a walnut!

Find out more ➤ Dinosaurs 48   Living things 91

Dinosaurs

Life in the Past

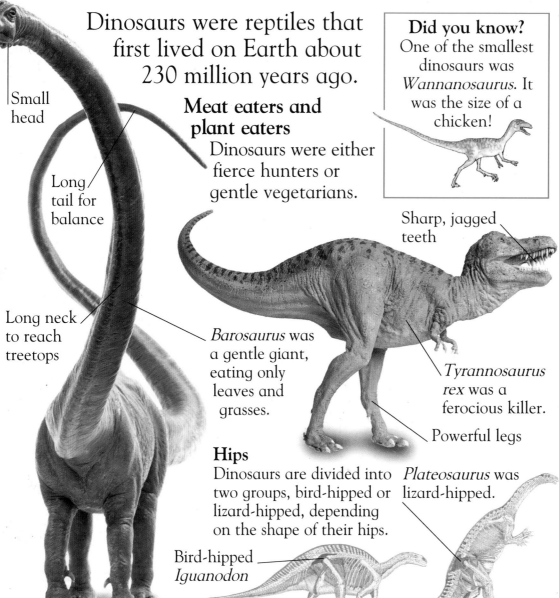

Dinosaurs were reptiles that first lived on Earth about 230 million years ago.

Small head

Long tail for balance

Long neck to reach treetops

Meat eaters and plant eaters
Dinosaurs were either fierce hunters or gentle vegetarians.

Barosaurus was a gentle giant, eating only leaves and grasses.

Sharp, jagged teeth

Tyrannosaurus rex was a ferocious killer.

Powerful legs

Hips
Dinosaurs are divided into two groups, bird-hipped or lizard-hipped, depending on the shape of their hips.

Plateosaurus was lizard-hipped.

Bird-hipped *Iguanodon*

Did you know?
One of the smallest dinosaurs was *Wannanosaurus*. It was the size of a chicken!

Changing Earth

The dinosaur age lasted so long that scientists have split it into three parts.

Dinosaurs first appeared 245 million years ago in the **Triassic period**.

In the **Jurassic period**, 208 million years ago, many new dinosaurs appeared.

Dinosaurs died out 65 million years ago at the end of the **Cretaceous period**.

Fossils
Scientists learn about dinosaurs by studying fossils found in the ground.

Struthiomimus

Model of dinosaur nest

Crocodile

Fossilized bones tell us the shape of these extinct animals.

Fossilized egg

Fossilized skin shows that some dinosaurs were covered in scales like reptiles of today, such as crocodiles.

Find out more Dinosaur types 47　　Fossils 74

Life in the Past

Early humans

Tools and weapons

Fire sticks

A **stone adze** was used to cut wood or dig up roots.

Diggers were sticks used to dig up grubs from the ground.

A **leather shoulder bag** carried a hunter's bow and arrows.

Arrowheads and blades were made from a hard stone called flint.

Arrows

About 30,000 years ago, people began to shelter in caves, gather their own food, and make tools from wood and stone.

Fire
Fire kept people warm, cooked their food, and frightened wild animals away.

Dry wood or grass

Cave painting
Early artists painted pictures of animals on cave walls.

Rubbing sticks together made a spark. This set fire to the grass.

Bread made from grains

Clothing
Clothes were made from wool and hairy animal skins.

Wool

Animal skin

Dyes from plants

Food
People hunted animals, dug up roots, and gathered seeds for food.

Salmon

Deer

Nuts and berries

Bronze age
Bronze was first used about 5,000 years ago to make metal objects.

Sickle to cut crops

Pin

Belt decoration

Neck ring

Iron age
Iron is a harder metal than bronze. It was first made about 4,000 years ago.

Bracelet

Razor

Brooch

Dagger

Did you know?
Early humans met and knew only about 25 people in their entire lifetime!

Find out more ➤ Fossils 74    Materials 97

49

Earth

The atmosphere

The atmosphere is made up of several different layers.

The highest layer is 430 miles (700 km) above the Earth. Satellites fly here.

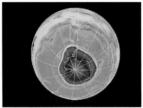

The ozone layer contains ozone gas, which protects Earth from the Sun's rays.

The middle layer is up to 30 miles (50 km) high. Planes fly here, above the clouds.

The lowest layer is only 7 miles (10 km) high. It contains the gases we need to live.

The Earth is a giant rocky ball spinning in space. It is surrounded by the atmosphere – layers of air that protect the planet and provide the oxygen we need to breathe.

Inside the Earth

The Earth is made up of different layers of rock and metal.

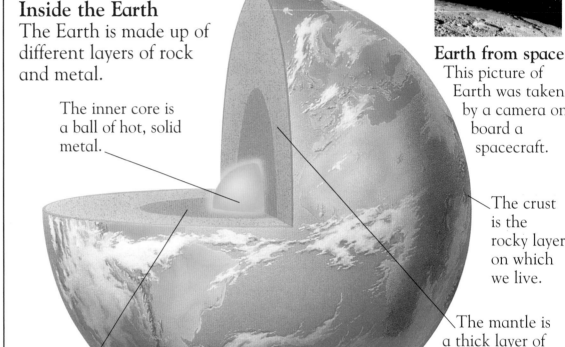

The inner core is a ball of hot, solid metal.

The outer core is a very thick liquid metal.

Earth from space

This picture of Earth was taken by a camera on board a spacecraft.

The crust is the rocky layer on which we live.

The mantle is a thick layer of rock. It is very hot and some of it moves slowly.

Earth's ingredients

The **crust** is made up of basalt and granite.

The **mantle** is a mix of metals like peridotite.

The **core** is made of solid metals like iron.

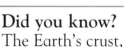

Basalt   Granite   Peridotite   Iron

Water and ice cover over three-quarters of the Earth's surface.

The **atmosphere** is made up of colorless gases that surround the Earth.

Did you know?

The Earth's crust, when compared to the whole of the Earth, is thinner than the skin of an apple.

Find out more

 Planets 109

Rocks and minerals 120

World of Nature

Eggs and nests

Birds and insects, frogs and snakes – most animals lay eggs. But some animals build nests especially to protect their eggs and babies.

Types of eggs

Butterfly eggs are laid on leaves and look like tiny jewels.

Frogs lay hundreds of eggs, protected by a jelly, in water.

Tortoise eggs are soft and leathery and buried in sand.

Hens' eggs are soft at first, but harden quickly as they dry.

Dogfish lay their tough egg cases among seaweed.

Slugs lay clear eggs in damp places, such as under a log.

Bird's nest

Birds collect all sorts of materials to make a warm, comfortable home like this wagtail's nest.

Moss for warmth

Did you know ?
Red-billed hornbills make nests in hollow trees and seal off the entrance until their chicks hatch.

Feathers for warmth

String

Mud mixed with spit

Twigs for structure

Shiny foil

Lichen for camouflage

Horse hair

Unusual nests

Male **weaver birds** use their beaks and claws to weave wonderful nests of grass.

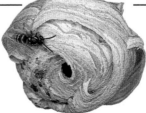

Wasp nests are made from chewed-up wood and feel like paper.

Quails scrape nests among rocks and dirt, so their brown speckled eggs will blend in.

Electricity

Did you know?
One flash of lightning has the same power as 50 million batteries!

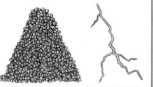
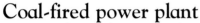

Electricity is a kind of energy. It is useful because it can be made easily, then sent into homes where it provides heat, light, and power.

Coal

Fuel
Coal, oil, and gas are all used in power plants.

Oil

Gas

Types of energy
Different types of energy can be used to make electricity.

Hydroelectric dams use the power of running water to make electricity.

Coal-fired power plant
Power plants burn coal to heat water and make steam. The steam turns turbines, which produce electricity.

Turbines in the main building are powered by steam.

Steam escapes through chimneys.

Solar power uses the sun's light rays to produce electricity.

Wind turbines have huge sails that turn in the wind, helping make electricity.

Tower
From the power plant, electricity is transported along wire cables supported by towers.

Electricity cable
In towns, most cables are buried underground. A few are carried on small poles.

Lightning
Lightning is a kind of electricity. It is as natural as wind and rain.

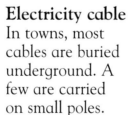

Battery power
Batteries contain chemicals that make electricity. Batteries are used to power things like toys and flashlights.

Battery
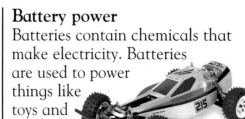

Battery-run car

Nuclear power plants use chemical reactions to make electricity.

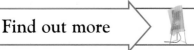
Find out more ➤ Electricity at home 53   Oil 106

Electricity at home

In the kitchen

Ovens often use electricity to heat up and cook our food.

Microwaves run on electricity. They cook food very quickly.

Refrigerators use electricity to keep food cool and fresh.

It's hard to imagine life without electricity. We use it to heat and light our homes, cook our food, listen to music, and talk on the phone.

Light
Electric lighting is bright and safe. It replaced candles and gas lamps, used in the past.

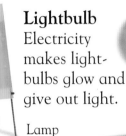

Lightbulb
Electricity makes lightbulbs glow and give out light.

Lamp

Did you know?
Most lightbulbs last about 1,000 hours – all day and night for a month!

At night, lights shine out in the dark.

Electric plug
Electricity flows along wires and into the plugs in wall sockets.

Safety in the home
Electricity can be very dangerous.

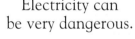

Never touch damaged wires.

Entertainment

Televisions use electricity to make sounds and pictures.

Computers are powerful machines. They use very little electricity.

Telephones use electricity to change our voices into signals.

Never use electrical objects near water.

Energy

A person running, a fire burning, a plant growing – all these things use energy. Energy makes things happen. Without it, there would be no life on Earth.

Sun
The sun provides the energy all living things need.

People and energy
Your body needs energy for everything you do – whether you're thinking, working, or running.

Runners use up huge amounts of energy.

Athletes eat high-energy foods.

Types of energy
Energy comes in many forms.

Heat energy can be used to cook food and keep us warm.

Light energy can come from a flame, electric light or the sun.

Sound energy is produced when something vibrates.

Food for energy
People and animals get energy from the food they eat. Some foods give us more energy than others.

Calories
The energy value of food is measured in calories. Pasta has more calories and gives us more energy than carrots.

Pasta

Carrot

Chemical energy is stored in plants. Animals eat the plants and use the energy.

Did you know?
Old animal droppings can be a source of energy. They give off a gas that burns.

Machines
All machines need energy to work. A car gets energy from burning fuel, but a bike gets its energy from you!

Energy supplies

Oil

Gas   Coal

Oil, coal, and gas are all sources of energy. But these fuels will run out one day.

Electrical energy is the main source of power in modern homes.

Find out more  Food and eating 70   Oil 106

Europe

Central Europe

The area of central Europe covers many countries. It is is a region of flat farmland, wooded hills, and snowcapped mountains.

Did you know?
- Wild pigs called boars still live in the forests of central Europe.
- The Rhine River is 820 miles (1,320 km) long – the length of the UK.

Rhine River
The Rhine is an important riverway for transporting cargo across the region.

Netherlands
The low-lying land by the sea is flat and fertile – perfect for growing bulbs.

European bison
Bison once lived in huge herds. Now they are protected.

Map labels:
Elbe River
POLAND
AMSTERDAM
NETHERLANDS
BERLIN
WARSAW
Lek River
Odra River
GERMANY
BELGIUM
BRUSSELS
Rhine River
ARDENNES
Vistula River
PRAGUE
CZECH REPUBLIC
CARPATHIAN MOUNTAINS
LUXEMBOURG
SLOVAKIA
Capital cities
1 LUXEMBOURG
2 VADUZ
Danube River
BLACK FOREST
VIENNA
BRATISLAVA
Danube River
BUDAPEST
ALPS
AUSTRIA
BERN
SWITZERLAND
HUNGARY
Mount Eiger
LIECHTENSTEIN
N

Carpathian Mountains
These mountains lie to the east of Europe.

Mount Eiger
Mount Eiger is one of the highest peaks in the Alps.

The Ardennes
This is an area of hills and valleys in southern Belgium.

Black Forest
The Black Forest in Germany is an area of wooded mountains.

Danube River
This river runs through six countries in central Europe.

Find out more Mammals of the world 95 Rivers and lakes 119

Europe: culture

Did you know?
St. Bernard dogs are trained to find people who are lost in the mountains.

Central Europe
Central Europe has a large population. Many of the people live in busy, crowded cities.

Winter sports
Many people go to the Austrian and Swiss Alps to enjoy the winter sports.

Skiing

Regional food

Root vegetables, such as beetroot and potatoes, are grown in Poland.

Mussels and chips is a popular dish. This dish is often eaten in Belgium.

Prague
The capital of the Czech Republic has some of the most beautiful architecture in Europe.

Opera house

The Old Town Bridge Tower

Vltava River

Swiss chocolate is made with the milk from Switzerland's famous dairy herds.

Edam cheese is traditionally made in the Netherlands.

Pretzels are made from wheat. They are popular in Germany.

Industry
Germany manufactures cars for countries all over the world.

Regional products

Cuckoo clocks and watches are made in Switzerland.

Tulips
Tulips are flown all around the world from the Netherlands.

National costume
Poland's national costume is worn for celebrations.

Architecture
The architecture of central Europe is highly decorative, such as this church in Vienna.

Find out more Sports of the world 136 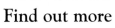 Towns and cities 140

Continents of the World

Europe

Northern Europe
This cool, wet region has snowy mountains and pine forests in the north, and rolling hills in the south.

Pine forest
The tough northern pine forests survive the bitterly cold winters.

Hot springs
In Iceland, hot springs, called geysers, spurt out of the ground.

Fjord
Norway's fjords are deep inlets carved into the coastline by rivers of ice.

ICELAND
• REYKJAVIK

Cotswolds
The English landscape has many gently rolling hills, but no high mountains.

Scottish highlands
Scotland is a land of rugged mountains and beautiful lakes.

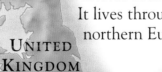

Rhododendron
This evergreen plant survives cold winters. It lives throughout northern Europe.

HIGHLANDS
SCOTLAND

NORTHERN
IRELAND

REPUBLIC
OF IRELAND
• DUBLIN

UNITED
KINGDOM

WALES   ENGLAND

COTSWOLDS

LONDON •

Red squirrel
Red squirrels live in forests, feeding on nuts and seeds.

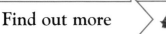

N

Lake Inari

F I N L A N D

Lake Oulu

N O R W A Y

S W E D E N

HELSINKI •

• TALLINN

ESTONIA

OSLO •

STOCKHOLM •

Lake Vänern

RIGA •

LATVIA

LITHUANIA

COPENHAGEN •
DENMARK

VILNIUS •

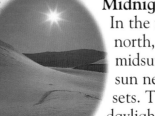

Midnight sun
In the far north, the midsummer sun never sets. There is daylight even at night!

Did you know?
• In Iceland there is so much hot water under the ground that it is used to heat whole towns.
• There are more than 100,000 lakes in Sweden.

Find out more ▷ Climates 39   Forests 73

57

Continents of the World

Europe: culture

Northern Europe

The industrial countries of northern Europe still have strong traditions of farming and fishing.

Tea
The British are famous for drinking tea.

Big Ben clock tower

London
London is the capital of the United Kingdom. It is a modern city with many historic buildings.

Houses of Parliament

London bus

Regional products

Cheese   Butter

Dairy products are widespread in northern Europe, especially in Ireland.

Lego is a world-famous toy from Denmark.

Timber from the region's forests is sold around the world.

Rugby
Rugby is a popular sport throughout the United Kingdom.

Fishing
Many of the countries in this region have large fishing fleets.

Aircraft, such as this Concorde, are produced all over the United Kingdom.

Culture

Tartan is a traditional Scottish material.

Wooden stave churches were once built in Norway.

Smörgasbord is a cold buffet, served in Sweden.

Sami
The Sami people live a traditional life, herding reindeer in Lapland.

Find out more Fish of the world 68   Sports 135

Continents of the World

Europe

Southern Europe

Southern Europe stretches down to the Mediterranean Sea. It is a dry, hilly land, with hot summers and mild winters.

Did you know?
- Huge flocks of flamingos fly to southern Europe in the summer months.
- There are 36 villages built on the slopes of the active volcano Mount Etna.

Provence
Wild herbs grow in the hills of Provence in southern France.

Alps
The Alps are the longest and highest mountain range in Europe.

Alpine flower
The bird's-eye primrose flowers in early summer.

Meseta Plain
The Meseta Plain lies in the middle of Spain. It is a high, rocky area with very few trees.

The Camargue
This French saltmarsh is famous for its wild horses.

Rock of Gibraltar
This rocky cliff lies at the tip of Spain. It is home to the only monkeys in Europe.

Mount Etna
Mount Etna is an active volcano on the island of Sicily. It last erupted in 1995.

Greek islands
Greece is a hot, dry land with hundreds of small islands in a warm, blue sea.

Olive tree
Olive trees grow on the dry southern hills.

Map labels: PARIS, Seine River, Loire River, FRANCE, MASSIF CENTRAL, PROVENCE, Camargue, MONACO, ANDORRA LA VELLA, ANDORRA, Ebro River, Duero River, PORTUGAL, LISBON, SPAIN, MADRID, MESETA PLAIN, Rock of Gibraltar, Corsica, Sardinia, ALPS, Po River, San Marino, ITALY, ROME, Sicily, Mount Etna, SLOVENIA, LJUBLJANA, CROATIA, ZAGREB, BOSNIA AND HERZEGOVINA, SARAJEVO, BELGRADE, YUGOSLAVIA, MACEDONIA, SKOPJE, TIRANA, ALBANIA, GREECE, ATHENS, Greek Islands, SOFIA, BULGARIA, ROMANIA, BUCHAREST, MOLDOVA, CHISINAU

N

Find out more Flowers 69 Mountains 99

Continents of the World

Europe: culture

Southern Europe
These countries are rich in history, and are world famous for their good food and wonderful wines.

Did you know?
Vatican City is the smallest state in the world.

Vatican City, Rome
Vatican City, in Rome, is the head-quarters of the Catholic Church.

Industry
Wine is made from grapes throughout this region.

Cork is made from the bark of the cork oak tree, which grows in Portugal.

Grand Piazza — St. Peter's Basilica

Beaches on the Mediterranean coast attract many tourists to southern Europe.

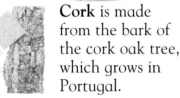

Tourism
Ancient ruins, such as the temple of Apollo in Greece, are popular with tourists.

Fishing
Fishing is very important in Greece. The seas contain squid, sardines, and tunny fish.

Architecture

Châteaux are old castles that were built in France about 400 years ago.

Orthodox churches in Greece are richly decorated on the inside.

Greek houses have white walls to reflect the heat of the sun in summer.

Ancient buildings, like this tower, are found in Portugal.

Food
Southern Europe has many famous foods and dishes that are eaten worldwide.

Olive oil   Oranges   Paella   Cheese   Lamb kebabs   Pasta

Find out more 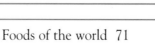 Foods of the world 71   Homes and houses 78

Life in the Past

Explorers

For thousands of years people have explored the world, hoping to find fertile farmland, fine goods, and riches.

Travelers

Pacific islanders were the first to cross the Pacific Ocean.

The **Vikings** sailed to the south to find fertile farmland.

Viking helmet

Merchants explored the route between China and Europe to trade in silk.

Arabs traveled in the 13th century to trade and find new lands.

Columbus, a Spanish explorer, crossed the Atlantic Ocean using an astrolabe.

Sailing ship
Starting in the 1400s, European sailors explored the world in fast, sturdy ships like this one.

Four masts for large sails

Sailors spotted land from the crow's nest.

Room for cargo, food, and water

Round Earth

In 1519 a famous Spanish explorer, Magellan, sailed around the world – and proved that it was round.

Ship's compass

Finding the way
Explorers used the sun, stars, and instruments to find their way.

Sextant

Backstaff

Telescope

Goods

Explorers brought home new foods and riches from around the world.

Jade

Cloves

Cinnamon

Pineapple

Did you know?
Before the 1520's, most people thought the world was flat!

Find out more ➤  Vikings 145   Ships and boats 127

Science and Technology

Factories

Clothes, chocolate, cars – almost everything we buy is mass produced in factories. Factories use machines to make goods in the thousands.

1 Raw materials
All the chocolate ingredients are sent to the factory.

Sugar   Milk   Cocoa pods

Types of factories

A **hat factory** makes thousands of hats in one style at a time.

Chocolate factory
A chocolate factory is organized so that chocolate bars can be made quickly and cheaply.

2 Production process
Machines make the chocolate, pour it into molds, and wrap it when it's cold and hard.

Chocolate bars on conveyor belt

Chocolate is checked for quality.

Washing machine factories have testing facilities to ensure quality.

Computer factories make hundreds of new computers on a conveyor belt.

Car factories use robots to put cars together.

3 Finished product
The finished chocolate bars are packed and shipped to stores, ready for you to buy.

Chocolate bar

Leather goods
This shoe factory uses the leftover shoe leather to make other goods, such as wallets and key rings.

Food factories keep their machines very clean, so that the food is safe to eat.

Find out more ▷ Computers 42   South America: culture 132

Life Today

Farm animals

Types of cattle farming

Hereford bull

Some cattle are farmed for meat.

Jersey cow

Others are farmed for their milk.

Fish farming

Trout and salmon are raised on fish farms. The farms provide cheap fish.

Farmers have kept and raised animals for thousands of years. They provide people with food and other useful materials.

Sheep
Farmers around the world keep sheep for their meat, milk, and soft, warm wool. The sheep are kept in flocks.

Sheep's milk

Wool is used to make clothing, fabrics, and carpets.

Warm coat in winter

Sheep shearing

Wool comes off in one piece called a fleece.

Sheep's cheese

Short coat keeps sheep cool in summer.

Sheep's wool is warm and oily.

Types of farm animals

Llamas provide milk, meat, leather, and wool.

Turkeys are bred for their meat.

Ostriches are farmed for their skin, meat, and feathers.

Pigs are farmed for their meat and leather.

Free-range farming
Free-range farming allows farm animals to wander around freely.

Intensive farming
Some farmers keep animals indoors in small pens. This is called intensive farming.

Find out more Australasia: culture 28 Farming 64

Life Today

Farming

Most of the food that we buy each day in stores is grown on farms throughout the world.

In some countries, farmers use rice harvesters to gather rice quickly.

Rice farming
Most rice is grown in parts of Asia where the weather is warm and wet.

Rice plants grow in water.

More than half the world's people live on rice.

Flooded rice fields are called paddy fields.

Most of the work is done by hand.

Did you know?
In southern Europe, farmers use pigs to find mushrooms called truffles.

Rice products

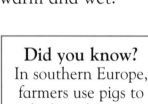
Fried rice

Rice cakes

Noodles

Rice paper

Farm tools and machines

Ox-drawn plows slowly break up soil for planting.

Tractors are expensive, but powerful. This one is sowing seeds.

Crop sprayers spray chemicals over plants to protect them from pests.

Pitchforks are an old farm tool. They are used to pick up hay.

Scythes are used to harvest crops by hand. The blade is very sharp.

Combine harvesters gather cereal crops quickly and efficiently.

Farm crops
Vegetables are grown outside in fields and inside in greenhouses.

Squash

Sugar beet

Fruits grow on plantations, in orchards, and in fields.

Apples

Cape gooseberry

Corn

Cereals, such as wheat and corn, are grown in huge fields around the world.

Wheat

Find out more ▷ Asia: culture 21   Foods of the world 71

Life Today

Festivals

Festivals are special days in the year when people celebrate and remember events in the past.

Festival customs

Candles are a symbol of life and truth.

March to May

In **Holy Week** Christians remember when Jesus died and was resurrected.

Mardi Gras

Mardi Gras is a festival in Brazil. Christians used to celebrate this day before beginning a 40-day fast.

June to August

The **summer solstice** has been celebrated for 4,000 years. People gather to watch the sunrise on Midsummer's Day.

September to November

Halloween was once a time to scare away evil spirits. Today it is a day of fun.

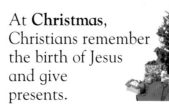

On **Thanksgiving,** families celebrate the harvest season with a special meal.

Colorful costumes

Dancing crowds

December to February

At **Chinese New Year** a dragon dances through the streets, chasing away the past.

At **Christmas,** Christians remember the birth of Jesus and give presents.

Costumes often have special meanings. They may be a disguise.

Music helps people have fun together.

Dances are a way of reliving customs of the past.

Did you know?

On March 1, Greeks smash pitchers against their front doors to get rid of mice and fleas.

Find out more ➤   Ancient China 12   Religion 115

Film

Life Today

Films tell stories using moving pictures, sound, and special effects to create great entertainment.

Clapper board

Film set
It takes a large team of people, and a lot of money, to make a film.

Microphones pick up every sound.

Camera

Film history

Silent films were the first films. They were in black and white.

Engineers control the lighting.

The director is in charge.

Actors

Talkies appeared in 1927. People flocked to the cinema to hear actors speak.

Color films were a hit when they arrived in the 1930s.

Types of films
Millions of people go to the theater to see many different types of films.

Science fiction

Western

Horror

Special-effects use the latest computer technology.

Cartoon
Cartoon films are made up of many drawings, which move when run together.

Find out more ▷ Asia: culture 25   Computers 42

Fish

World of Nature

Fish live in the world's rivers, lakes, and oceans. The way fish look, move, and breathe is perfectly suited to their underwater life.

Did you know?
Male catfish carry the females' eggs inside their mouths until they hatch.

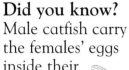

Fins help fish steer.

Tail fin works like a paddle

Goldfish
A fish's body is smooth and streamlined, just like this goldfish. It is the perfect shape for moving quickly through water.

Gills

Eye

Scaly skin

Fin

Defense

A school of dart fish is harder to attack than one fish on its own.

Long spines make the pufferfish almost impossible to swallow!

Camouflage helps flounders blend in with the seabed.

Types of fish

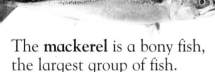

The **mackerel** is a bony fish, the largest group of fish.

Lampreys are part of a small group called jawless fish.

This **leopard shark** is a member of the shark group.

Breathing
Fish breathe underwater with their gills. These take oxygen from the water as the fish swims along.

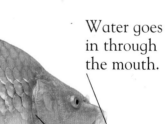

Water goes in through the mouth.

Water comes out of the gills.

Eggs
Most fish lay millions of jellylike eggs straight into the water. This is called spawning.

Torpedo rays give an electric shock when they are attacked.

Find out more ▷ Fish of the world 68   Sea animals 123

Fish of the world

There are more than 30,000 different kinds of fish in the world today. Just over half of them live in salty seawater. The others live in freshwater lakes, rivers, and streams.

Did you know?
Not all fish live in water. Mudskippers spend a lot of time on land, even up trees!

Stickleback
Sticklebacks live in the northern Atlantic Ocean. They feed on smaller fish.

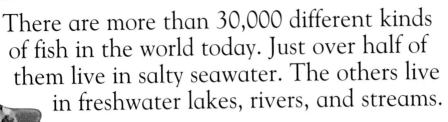

Leopard shark
This harmless shark lives and hunts in the Pacific Ocean.

Tiger barb
This tiny, striped fish lives in streams and rivers on warm Pacific islands.

European eel
These eels live in European rivers, but travel far out into the ocean to breed.

Queen angelfish
This tropical fish lives in the coral reefs of the Pacific Ocean. Its coloring helps it hide in the coral.

Piranha
Piranhas are deadly hunters. They live in the rivers of South American rain forests.

Where fish live

Tench

Ocean deep
Only a few fish can survive in the cold, dark water in the deepest parts of the ocean.

Seas and oceans
Many saltwater fish live near the surface. Some swim in schools deeper down. Still others lie on the seabed itself.

Butterflyfish

Angler fish

Rivers and lakes
Freshwater fish are often more colorful than the fish of the sea. Different kinds choose to live in still or fast-flowing water.

Tropical seas
The warm, shallow tropical seas are home to some of the world's most beautiful fish.

Cod

Find out more ➤ 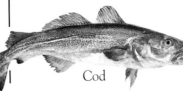 Fish 67   Rivers and lakes 119

Flowers

We love flowers for their color, shape, and scent. Yet their loveliness is not for us; it's to attract small creatures to visit them.

Did you know?

The Venus's-flytrap gets extra food by trapping and digesting small insects!

Lily

Flowers can look very different from each other, but they all have the same basic parts – just like this lily.

Petal

Petals come in many shapes, sizes, and colors to attract insects and birds, which pollinate the flowers.

Petal

Patterns lead insects to the center.

Rose

Perfume

Many flowers have a sweet smell and are used to make soaps, oils, and perfumes.

The sticky stigma collects pollen from other lily plants.

Stamens make a fine yellow dust called pollen.

Pollination

Pollen must be carried from one flower to another to make seeds.

1 A bee visits a flower to feed on its sweet nectar.

2 As the bee feeds, pollen on the stamens sticks to its legs.

3 At the next flower, the pollen brushes onto the stigma.

4 This flower is now pollinated, and can begin to make seeds.

Unusual flowers

Water lily flowers float on water.

Grasses have dull flowers.

Urn plants have red flowers to attract birds.

Catkins are groups of tiny flowers found on some trees.

Find out more Fruits and seeds 75   Plants 110

Science and Technology

Food and eating

To stay strong and healthy, it is important to eat the right foods. Food gives us energy – plus it's delicious to eat!

A good diet
The food you eat makes your diet. A healthy diet has food from five different groups. Each group helps your body in a different way.

Proteins help the body grow and repair itself. They are found in meat, fish, dairy products, and nuts.

Vitamins and minerals in fresh fruits and vegetables help fight disease.

Fat is found in oil, butter, and avocados, and is stored in the body for extra energy.

Preserving food

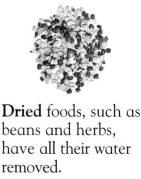

Dried foods, such as beans and herbs, have all their water removed.

Pickled foods, such as fruits and vegetables, are preserved in vinegar or a sugary syrup.

Canned foods, like fruit, fish, and meat, are packed in liquid in a sealed can.

Frozen foods, such as meat, fish, and vegetables, keep well for several months.

Digestion
1 From your mouth, food goes to your stomach.

2 Your stomach juices turn the food into liquid.

3 The liquid is squeezed along the intestines. Here the nutrients pass into your blood.

4 The leftovers are pushed out when you use the bathroom.

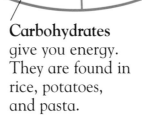

Carbohydrates give you energy. They are found in rice, potatoes, and pasta.

Water
Your body needs about 5 pints (3 liters) of water every day.

Fiber helps food move through your intestines. Cereals, nuts, beans, and bread all contain fiber.

Smoked foods, such as fish and bacon, are dried, or cured, in a room full of smoke.

Find out more  Farming 64   Foods of the world 71

Foods of the world

Pineapples, peanuts, and pears –
our food comes from all over the
world, adding color, flavor,
and variety to our diet.

Did you know?
Every day humans
eat a pile of rice more
than six times the size
of the Great Pyramid!

Wheat
Canada has the
ideal climate for
wheat, which
needs a wet spring
and a dry summer.

Olive oil
Olives grow in the
hot, dry climate of
southern Europe.
Olives are squeezed
to make oil.

Root vegetables
Root vegetables, such as
turnips, grow well
in the cool, wet
climate of
northern Asia.

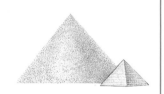

Tea
Tea plants grow in
warm, wet, and hilly
areas throughout
Southeast Asia.

Bananas
Bananas grow in
a hot, tropical
climate, like
that of South
America.

Chocolate
Chocolate is
made from the
beans of the cacao
tree. These grow in hot,
wet African rain forests.

Peaches
Peaches are grown
in Australia,
where there are
cool springs and
hot summers.

Transporting food

Planes are used
to transport
fruits and
vegetables.
Fresh food,
like oranges,
rots if it is
not eaten
quickly.

Orange grove

Fishing boats far from
land pack the fish they
catch in ice. This keeps
the fish fresh until the
boat returns to shore.

Trucks carry dried foods,
like spices, to a market.
Dried foods
keep well.

Find out more   Asia: culture 25   Food and eating 70

World of Nature

Forest animals

Did you know?
Wolves pull faces to show other wolves how they are feeling: angry, sad, or happy!

The forest makes a wonderful home for animals. The trees provide them with everything they need – food, hiding places, and shelter from the cold.

Squirrel
Squirrels feed on nuts, cones, and insects.

Badger
Badgers live in underground burrows. They hunt at night.

Forest mini-beasts

Earthworms drag dead leaves under the soil, which makes it more fertile.

Forest birds

Woodpeckers
drill holes into trees to make nests and eat insects under the bark.

Raccoon
Raccoons climb trees to steal eggs from nests.

Powerful jaws tear out tough roots.

Grizzly bear
Bears feed on plants, tree roots, and small animals. They are well adapted to forest life.

Wood ants live in colonies of up to 100,000 ants. They eat other insects.

Crossbills have
twisted beaks, which they use to open cones.

Jays feed on seeds, but they also steal eggs from other birds' nests.

Thick fur to keep warm

Strong claws can dig out roots and grip trees.

Strong legs for climbing trees

Millipedes
scurry through the leaves on the forest floor.

Weevils
help break down dead plants.

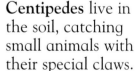

Tawny owls spend all day hiding in a tree, then come out to hunt at night.

Centipedes live in the soil, catching small animals with their special claws.

Find out more 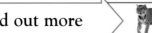 Animals in danger 18 Forests 73

World of Nature

Forests

Forests grow in many different parts of the world. There are three main types of forests: coniferous, deciduous, and rain forest.

Deciduous forest

A deciduous forest contains a mix of different trees. Most of them lose their leaves in the fall, and grow new ones in the spring.

Horse chestnut leaf

Fall leaf color

Trees are a rounded shape.

Variety of trees

Oak leaf in fall

Maple leaf in fall

Leaves
The broad, flat leaves change color in the fall.

Oak leaf

Mountain ash blossom

Blossom
Trees grow flowers to attract insects.

Seeds
Seeds often grow inside a tasty fruit.

Mountain ash berries

Deciduous forest plants

Mushrooms help decompose dead plants, keeping soil fertile for growth.

Primroses bloom in the spring, before the leaves on the trees block out the sun.

Mosses are small, flowerless plants that grow in damp places.

Bluebells cover the forest floor with a carpet of purple flowers.

Coniferous forest

Coniferous forests contain evergreen trees, which can survive very cold weather. Evergreens shed some needles all year round.

Snow slides off the branches.

Trees are a triangular shape.

Leaves
Leaves, called needles, are thin and tough.

Pine needles

Spruce cones

Pine cones

Poor, infertile soil

Cones
Seeds are protected inside a cone.

Did you know?
If polluted air mixes with rain, it can make acid rain. This harms forests by damaging the leaves on trees.

Find out more  Rain forests 114   Trees 143

World of Nature

Fossils

Fossils are the remains of plants and animals that lived millions of years ago. When discovered, they give us fascinating clues to the past.

Plant fossils

Mammoth
This huge mammal is now extinct. It was found frozen in the soil.

Shark's tooth
A tooth can tell scientists the size of an extinct animal.

Dung
This dropping came from a sharklike animal.

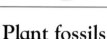

This **poplar leaf** fossil looks like poplar leaves today.

Ammonite
Ammonites were sea creatures that are now extinct.

Fin

Eye socket

These **seed** fossils are about 30 million years old.

Print of skeleton

Outline of soft tissue in rock

Ichthyosaur
This fossil of an extinct sea reptile was formed when the earth around it slowly turned into stone.

Early human skull
This fossilized skull teaches scientists about the first humans.

Bark fossils tell us which plants were growing millions of years ago.

Dinosaur footprint
This fossilized footprint shows how big and heavy its maker was.

Amber spider
This spider has been fossilized in amber, the juice of an ancient plant.

Did you know?
This man died 1,740 years ago, but his body was preserved in a peat bog in Denmark.

Fossil hunting
Only the simplest tools are needed to find fossils.

Fossils are very fragile. They must be uncovered very carefully.

A magnifying glass is useful to examine a fossil.

Find out more ➤ Dinosaurs 48   Rocks and minerals 120

Fruits and seeds

Different seeds
Seeds come in all shapes and sizes. They are protected in many different ways.

We think of fruits as juicy foods, like peaches and grapes. But fruits are really seed cases, and they certainly can't all be eaten!

Making seeds

1 As soon as a flower is pollinated, it starts to grow seeds.

Acorns are the fruit of the oak tree. Fruits that have hard, woody shells are called nuts.

Peas are seeds. They grow inside a fruit called a pea pod.

Dates are the fruits of palm trees. Each date contains one seed.

2 The petals drop off, leaving just a seed case.

Sycamore seeds grow inside a seed case that is wing-shaped.

Lemon seeds are called pips. They are protected by a fruit with juicy flesh and a tough skin.

Prickly pear seeds grow inside a thick, spiky-skinned fruit.

3 As the seeds grow, the seed case grows bigger, too. This is the fruit.

Spreading seeds
Seeds need to get away from their parent plant so that they will have plenty of room to grow.

Walkers carry seeds around in the mud on their boots.

4 The fruit ripens at the same time as the seeds inside.

Dandelion seeds float through the air on fluffy parachutes.

Did you know?
The world's largest seed is from the coco de la mer palm tree. It can weigh as much as 44 lb (20 kg).

Prickly burrs stick to animals' coats and are carried away.

Berries are eaten by birds, which leave the seeds in their droppings.

Coconuts float out to sea and are washed up on other beaches.

World of Nature

Grassland animals

Burrowing animals

Meerkats live in Africa in large groups under the ground.

Wild **guinea pigs** are found in South America. They live in the old burrows of other animals.

Wild **hamsters** live in Russia. To stay safe, they leave their burrows only at night.

Dingos are wild dogs that come from Australia. They live in other animals' burrows.

Many grassland animals have their food right under their feet! But life can be dangerous because there is nowhere to hide from predators.

Savanna animals
The savanna grasslands of Africa are home to huge herds of animals. They roam together looking for food and water.

Giraffes eat leaves off the scattered trees.

Wildebeests move around in huge herds. They are safer that way.

Did you know?
The fastest human runs 329 ft (100 m) in just under 10 seconds. But the cheetah can run it in 3.6 seconds!

Rhea
Rheas live in South America. They can't fly, but can run very fast from their enemies.

Echidna
Echidnas live in the Australian grasslands. In danger, they roll up, showing only their spikes.

Serval
Servals are wild cats that live in Africa. They run very fast and have excellent hearing.

Wallaby
Wallabies live and feed in the Australian grasslands. They can move very fast when in danger.

Secretary bird
Secretary birds have such long legs that they can walk through tall grasses. They live in Africa.

Find out more ⟩ Africa 6   Grasslands 77

W*orld of Nature*

Grasslands

Grasslands are vast, flat, grassy plains. Few trees grow there because it is too dry. Grasslands have different names around the world.

Prairies
The prairies lie in the center of North America. The fertile land has been turned into wheat fields.

Savanna
The tropical grasslands of Africa are called the savanna. The weather is warm, but very little rain falls.

Grasses
There are many kinds of grasses. But they are all very adaptable.

Grasses can dry out or even burn, but will grow back within hours of rain.

Grasses grazed by herds of animals

Small scrub tree

Flat, dry land

Pampas grasses have strong woody stems to keep them upright in strong wind.

Cereals are grasses grown on the prairies. They include corn and wheat, and are resistant to disease.

Pampas
The pampas of South America are used for cattle ranching. Cowboys on the pampas are called gauchos.

Mongolian nomad

Nomadic tent

Steppe
Steppe land exists across Asia. These cold, but fertile plains are home to nomads, who move with their animals in search of grazing land.

Did you know?
Bamboo is the fastest growing grass in the world. It can grow 3 ft (1 m) a day – the same height as a 2-year-old child.

Outback
In the dry Australian outback there are huge sheep farms called stations.

Life Today

Homes and houses

Home is where you live, eat, and sleep together as a family or alone. Homes give shelter from the weather.

Family house
Homes are often made of local materials suitable for the weather.

Bedrooms are upstairs.

Porch over front door

Wooden walls

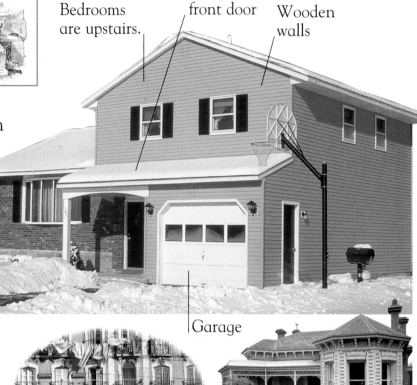

Garage

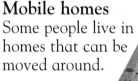

Apartment building
These have homes for lots of people.

Row houses
These houses lie near the center of many older cities.

Ranch house
Ranch houses have no stairs. They are built on one level.

Mobile homes
Some people live in homes that can be moved around.

Tepees and other tents are quick and easy to put up.

Campers are comfortable homes on wheels.

Houseboats are floating homes on a river or canal.

Caravans are homes pulled by horses or vehicles.

Homes of the world

Swiss chalets have sloping roofs to shed snow.

Greek homes often have white walls to reflect the Sun's heat.

New Guinean homes are built over lakes on stilts.

Nigerian homes are sometimes made of mud and straw.

Tunisian homes can be built underground to keep them cool.

Find out more Electricity at home 53   Towns and cities 140

Life Today

Hospitals and doctors

Hospitals are places where doctors and nurses care for people when they are sick or injured.

Accidents and emergencies

After an accident, patients are taken to the emergency room. Doctors examine them when they arrive.

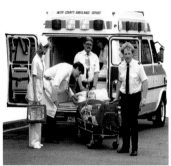

1 Ambulances take emergency patients to the hospital very quickly.

2 X rays show whether the patient has broken any bones.

Did you know?
In some countries, mobile hospitals visit patients instead of the other way around!

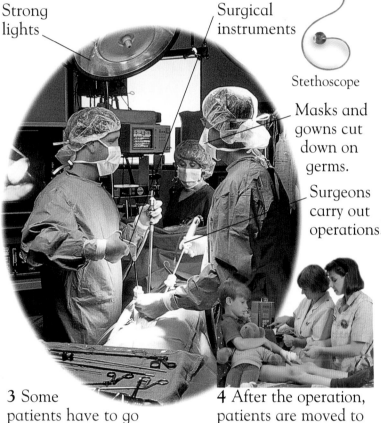

Strong lights

Surgical instruments

Stethoscope

Masks and gowns cut down on germs.

Surgeons carry out operations.

3 Some patients have to go to an operating room for surgery.

4 After the operation, patients are moved to a ward to rest and recover their strength.

Doctors at work

Doctors usually treat patients in an examing room.

Doctors sometimes treat people at the scene of an accident.

Doctors can give people health check-ups at work.

Doctors visit their most sick patients at home.

Some doctors have to fly to patients who live in remote areas.

Intensive care
Very sick patients may need special equipment to stay alive. This is called intensive care.

Nurses
Nurses care for patients both in hospitals and in homes.

Home-care nurse

Hospital nurse

Find out more ⇒ Human body: skeleton 82   Trucks 144

Human body: growth

From the moment our lives begin, our bodies are always changing. Our minds grow, too, as we learn more about the world around us.

Starting life

An **embryo** is a group of cells that grow into a baby inside the mother.

This **10-week-old fetus** has grown from the embryo.

This **five-month-old fetus** looks like a tiny human.

A **newborn baby** sucks milk from its mother.

Growing up
It takes about eighteen years to become a fully grown adult.

Young teenager

Fully grown adult

Baby

Elderly adult

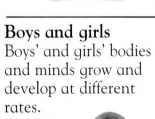

Child

Developing skills

Crawling starts at about 10 months.

Walking begins at about 15 months.

Speaking in full sentences begins at about two.

Writing starts at around the age of four or five.

Riding a bike is often mastered by the age of five or six.

Boys and girls
Boys' and girls' bodies and minds grow and develop at different rates.

Height
The height you reach largely depends on your parents. If they are both tall, it is likely that you will be tall, too.

Find out more ➤ Animals 17   Early humans 49

Science and Technology

Human body: senses

Sight, sound, touch, smell, and taste – your five senses tell your brain what is happening around you and help keep you safe.

The five senses

Touch
A rabbit is soft to the touch, but a hot pan can burn.

Sound
Sound lets us enjoy music. But it also warns us of danger, like a buzzing bee.

Touch

Sound

Working together
Your senses often work together. When you cross the road, you use your eyes to see and your ears to hear.

Taste

Taste
Taste tells you that ice cream is good to eat, but soap is not!

Sight
Your sight lets you thread a needle, and warns you not to touch a prickly cactus.

Sight

Smell

Smell
Your sense of smell lets you enjoy a rose. But it also warns you of sour milk or rotten eggs.

Sight problems
Guide dogs are trained to help blind or partially sighted people get around.

Braille is a form of writing that blind people "read" by touch.

Hearing problems
Sign language helps people who can't talk or hear communicate.

Hearing aids help people who can't hear well.

Did you know?
Our sight is so sharp we can see a candle flame 1 mile (1.6 km) away in the dark!

Human body: skeleton

Science and Technology

Skull protects your brain.

Shoulder blade

Rib cage protects your heart and lungs.

Spine

Elbow joint

Hip joint

Your hand has 27 bones.

Thigh-bones are the longest bones.

Kneecap

Shinbone

Ankle joint

Your foot has 26 bones.

Your skeleton has 208 bones! It gives you your human shape and protects your vital organs. Without bones and muscles, you couldn't move.

Bones
Bones are made of a hard, strong material called calcium. We get calcium from milk.

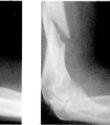

Broken bone X-ray pictures
If a bone breaks, a doctor may wrap it in a plaster cast. This helps the bone grow together.

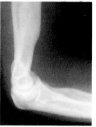

Long bones
Long bones are strong but light because they have air holes inside.

Inside of a bone, magnified thousands of times

Muscles
You have about 600 muscles. They work with your bones to help you move, skip, and jump.

Thigh muscle pulls on the bone, making your leg move.

How muscles work
All muscles work in pairs.

1 The biceps muscle pulls the arm up.

2 The triceps muscle pulls the arm down.

Did you know?
Every time you smile you use 17 muscles. But every time you frown you use 43.

Bone joints
Ball-and-socket joint at shoulder

Hinge joint

Joints are places where bones meet. They allow your body to bend.

False hip joint

False knee joint

False plastic joints are used to replace real joints if they wear out.

Biceps muscle

Triceps muscle

82

Science and Technology

Human body: skin

Your hair keeps in heat and protects your scalp.

Your made-to-measure skin is waterproof, elastic, and tough. It protects your body, keeping your insides in and harmful germs out.

Skin uses

Skin
Skin is dead on the outside. Dry specks brush off our bodies every day. New skin grows underneath.

Old age
As you become older, your skin begins to sag and wrinkle.

Skin is stretchy and moves when you do.

Hair
There are small hairs all over your body.

Skin contains tiny nerves that can sense touch.

Skin is waterproof. It protects you when you wash or go swimming.

If you are cold, the hairs on your skin stand up and trap air to keep you warm.

Eyebrows stop sweat from dripping into your eyes.

Sun-screen

Did you know?
Your skin weighs about 7 lbs (3 kg). That's as much as a small bag of potatoes!

When you are hot, your skin sweats salty water to cool you down.

Skin senses heat, cold, moisture, and pain.

Skin protection
It's important to protect your skin from the sun's harmful rays.

Hair
The hair on your head can come in any shape, length, and color. Hair helps keep you warm.

Fingerprint
The skin on everybody's fingertips has tiny ridges. These make unique patterns called fingerprints.

Find out more Insects of the world 87 Sports 135

83

Science and Technology

Human body: systems

Your body is a wonderful and complicated machine. It is made up of systems that work together to keep you alive.

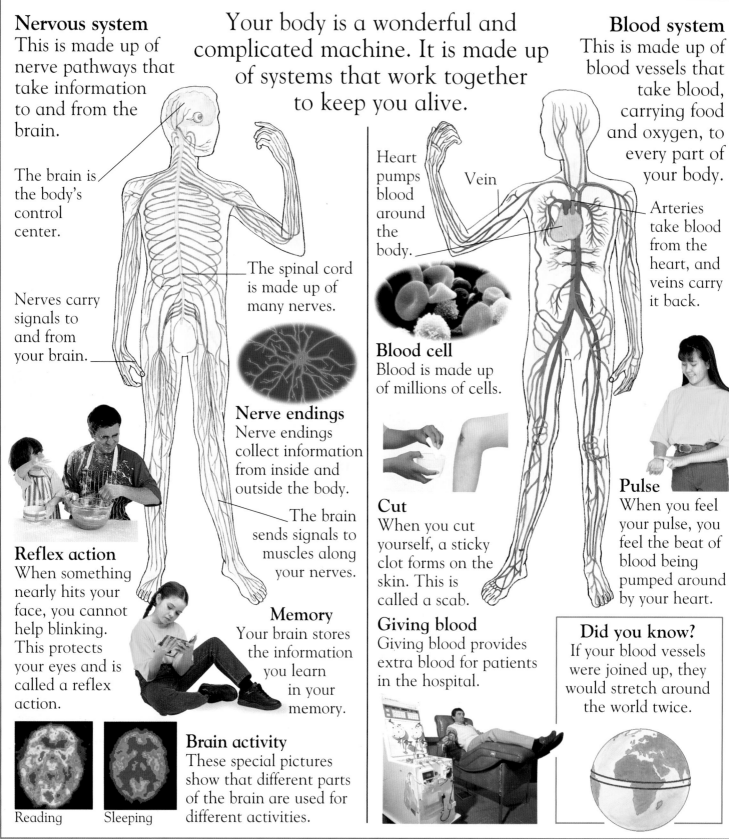

Nervous system
This is made up of nerve pathways that take information to and from the brain.

The brain is the body's control center.

Nerves carry signals to and from your brain.

The spinal cord is made up of many nerves.

Nerve endings
Nerve endings collect information from inside and outside the body.

The brain sends signals to muscles along your nerves.

Reflex action
When something nearly hits your face, you cannot help blinking. This protects your eyes and is called a reflex action.

Memory
Your brain stores the information you learn in your memory.

Brain activity
These special pictures show that different parts of the brain are used for different activities.

Reading   Sleeping

Blood system
This is made up of blood vessels that take blood, carrying food and oxygen, to every part of your body.

Heart pumps blood around the body.

Vein

Arteries take blood from the heart, and veins carry it back.

Blood cell
Blood is made up of millions of cells.

Cut
When you cut yourself, a sticky clot forms on the skin. This is called a scab.

Giving blood
Giving blood provides extra blood for patients in the hospital.

Pulse
When you feel your pulse, you feel the beat of blood being pumped around by your heart.

Did you know?
If your blood vessels were joined up, they would stretch around the world twice.

Find out more   Food and eating 70   Hospitals and doctors 79

Life in the Past

Incas

Inca toy
This pottery dog belonged to an Inca child.

Machu Picchu
The Incas were expert builders. This ancient city was built high up in the mountains of Peru.

The Incas were people who lived in South America more than 500 years ago. They ruled a great and wealthy empire.

Stone ruins of houses and temples

Flat terraces cut into the hillside.

Food grown on terraces.

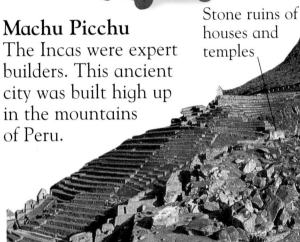

Inca life

Gold was used to make precious goods, such as this llama ornament.

Music
was very popular. These panpipes made a soft sound.

Religious ceremonies took place in special temples. Animals were often sacrificed.

Tools
Tools were made from wood, stone, bone, and wool.

Hoe for farming

Sling for hunting

Quinine for medicine

Plants
Plants were grown for food and medicine.

Potato

Corn

Snakeroot for stomach-ache

Llama
Llamas were used to carry goods up and down the mountains.

Gods and goddesses were important, such as this statue of the goddess of farming.

Dead bodies were carefully preserved. The Incas believed in life after death.

Did you know?
The Incas did not use writing. They recorded things on knotted strings called quipus.

Spanish conquest
When Spanish soldiers arrived in South America, they stole Incan gold and sent it back to Spain.

Spanish soldiers killed the Incan fighters quickly with their guns.

Helmet

Gun

 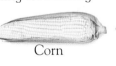

World of Nature

Insects

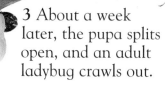

They crawl, fly, buzz, and sting – insects may be small, but there are over a million kinds, more than any other animal in the world.

Types of insects

Damselflies are expert fliers and dart through the air.

Beetles have hard wing cases to protect their delicate wings.

Flies have two wings that beat so fast they buzz.

Butterflies and moths have four patterned wings.

Did you know?
The South American grasshopper disguises itself as a thin twig.

Eyes

Antennae are feelers that taste and smell the air.

Tiny claws can hang on to plants.

Wasp
All insects have three sections to their bodies and six legs – just like this wasp.

The head is the first part of the body.

The thorax is the middle part of the body.

The abdomen is the end part of the body.

The six legs bend at the joints.

Wings

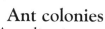

Ant colonies
Ants live in groups called colonies and share all the work to be done.

Growing up
Many insects change shape as they grow. This is called metamorphosis.

Ladybug

Ladybug egg

Larva

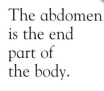

1 A wormlike larva hatches from an egg. It feeds and grows.

Pupa

2 The fully grown larva makes a hard case called a pupa around itself.

3 About a week later, the pupa splits open, and an adult ladybug crawls out.

Find out more Butterflies and moths 36 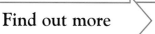 Insects of the world 87

World of Nature

Insects of the world

Insects live everywhere in the world except in the ocean. They make their homes in trees, in the ground, in buildings, and even on us!

American locust
A swarm of locusts may contain up to 10 billion insects. They will eat all the plants in their path.

Great diving beetle
This European pond dweller is fierce – it will even attack frogs.

Checkered skipper
This butterfly can survive in the freezing Arctic. It eats grass.

Did you know?
Whirlygig beetles have a set of upper eyes to see above water, and a set of lower eyes to keep watch underwater!

ARCTIC OCEAN

EUROPE

NORTH AMERICA

ASIA

ATLANTIC OCEAN

PACIFIC OCEAN

AFRICA

SOUTH AMERICA

INDIAN OCEAN

AUSTRALASIA

ANTARCTICA

Robber fly
This fly lives near beehives in South America. It kills bees in mid-air and eats them.

Asian violin beetle
This beetle is totally flat! It lives between thin layers of fungi on tree trunks.

Damselfly
This damselfly lives in southern Europe. It skims over water, feeding on flies.

Cockroach
Cockroaches live almost everywhere. They are scavengers and eat anything from paper to dead animals.

Head louse
This head louse, magnified many times, lives on human heads. It feeds on dead skin.

Praying mantis
This praying mantis lives in Africa and feeds on other insects. It grasps its prey between its two front legs.

Goliath beetle
The Goliath is the heaviest beetle in the world. It lives in the African rain forest, eating tropical fruit.

Find out more ▷   Human body: skin 83   Insects 86

Inventions

The wheel, X rays, computer games – inventions can change our lives, or simply be fun. They are new ideas that do a job in an original way.

Electricity
Many new inventions followed the discovery of electricity in 1831.

Electric heaters are more convenient than fires.

Electric light is safer than candlelight or gas lamps.

Electric irons were first used 100 years ago.

Communications
Modern inventions have helped people speak to each other over long distances.

Telephones send sounds along wires.

Satellite dishes send and receive messages from all around the world.

Transportation
The need to travel has led to many great inventions.

Axle

Wooden crossbar

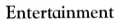

Cars first appeared about 100 years ago. Now millions of people drive.

Wheels are used on many kinds of vehicles. They were invented 5,000 years ago.

Planes were box-shaped at first. Today they are fast, large, and sleek.

Entertainment
Modern inventions have brought entertainment into the home.

Television is the most popular kind of home entertainment.

Computer games are often small and light, so they can be carried anywhere.

Compact discs play music that sounds as though it is playing live.

Medicine
Medical inventions help people live longer, healthier, and more active lives.

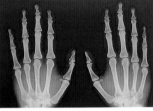

False teeth help people who have lost their real teeth eat.

X rays can help doctors see inside our bodies without cutting them open.

Stethoscopes, invented in 1855, are used to listen to our heart or lungs.

Did you know?
Thomas Edison, the inventor of the lightbulb, was expelled from school for laziness! (1847–1931)

Find out more Computers 42 Machines 92

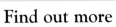

Knights

Knights were medieval soldiers in armor who fought on horseback for a lord or a king. They lived about 1,000 years ago.

Did you know?
A full suit of armor weighed about as much as a six-year-old child.

Weapons and armor
In battle, knights used dangerous weapons made of iron and steel. A suit of armor protected them from cuts and blows.

Horse armor
Some knights used armor for their horses, too.

Face guard

Neck guard

Spike

Eye guard

Nose guard

Spurs

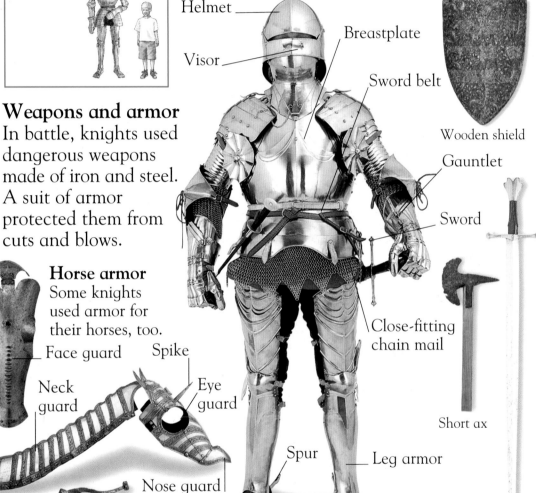

Helmet

Visor

Breastplate

Sword belt

Gauntlet

Sword

Close-fitting chain mail

Spur

Leg armor

Wooden shield

Short ax

Copper and steel sword

Types of armor

An **Italian knight** in 1380 had armor that covered only part of his body.

An **English knight** in 1590 was totally protected by his armor.

Samurai warriors were Japanese knights. Their metal armor was laced together with silk.

Tournaments
In times of peace, knights took part in jousting tournaments. They charged at each other on horseback, carrying lances.

Lance

Horses draped with knights' colors

Shield

Helmets
Tournaments were very colorful. Many knights wore unusual helmets.

Italian helmet

Helmet with eagle's beak

Find out more  Castles 38 Festivals 65

Light

Light rays
Light rays can travel through some materials.

Transparent
materials like glass allow light rays to travel through them.

Translucent

materials, such as plastics, let some light rays through.

Opaque
materials, like wrapping paper, do not let any light rays through.

Reflection
When light rays bounce off shiny things, like still water, they make a reflection.

It's impossible to think of a world without light. Light is a kind of energy that you can see. Without it, nothing can live or grow.

Light and shadow
Light travels in straight lines called rays. When light rays hit something solid, the light is blocked and a shadow forms on the other side.

The Sun is our planet's most important source of light.

Long shadow

Hand shadows
It's fun to make shadows with our hands.

Types of light

Electric light
is powered by electricity and used in buildings and outdoors.

Candlelight
was used to light homes in the past.

Glowworms
use special chemicals to make their light.

Lightning is a kind of electricity. It makes a flash of bright light.

Did you know?
People still tell the time by using the shadows on a sundial.

Plants and light
Plants need light to make food for themselves. They die if they are left in the dark.

Leaf in light   Leaf in dark

Plants grow toward light.

Fireworks explode to make a beautiful, chemical light.

Find out more ▷   Color 40   Sun and stars 137

Living things

Stones do not need air to breathe. They are not living.

Animals and plants are both living things. But there is one big difference – plants can make food for themselves, while animals have to find it.

Sunflower makes seeds

Animals
All animals move around to find food for themselves, just like this chicken.

Chicken breathes oxygen

Chickens have young called chicks.

Chickens peck the ground for food.

Plants
Like all plants, sunflowers are alive. They stay in one place and make food for themselves.

Plants use water, air, and sunlight to make their own food.

Sunflower is rooted in the ground

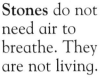

Moss

Corn

Dog

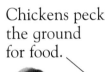

Spider

Sea urchin

Sponge

Bird

Cactus

Thistle

Seaweed

Did you know?
Coral may look like a lump of rock, but it is made of millions of tiny animals.

Ingredients for life

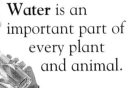

Water is an important part of every plant and animal.

Air helps plants and animals make energy for themselves.

Light helps plants grow. Without plants, animals would die from hunger.

Find out more ➤ Amphibians 11   Trees 143

Machines

Did you know?

The Greek scientist Archimedes invented a pulley that would allow one man to pull a ship in or out of water.

People have always used machines to make their lives easier. Simple machines like wheels, pulleys, and levers help us in dozens of ways every day.

Lever

Levers help lift loads. They have a rod or bar that turns around a pivot.

This corkscrew uses levers to lift a cork out of a bottle.

Pivot

Rod

Scissors are two levers joined together.

Bicycle

Bicycles are machines that use pedal power to carry us faster and farther than walking does.

Scales

This pair of scales is a lever.

Pivot

Rod

Pivot

Rod

The wheel spins around on the axle.

Gear

Gears are wheels with teeth that fit into each other. Gear wheels change the speed at which parts of a machine work.

Hand beater

The gears in a watch make the different hands move at different speeds.

Inside a watch

Gears give power on hills.

Pedals are levers to push against.

Wheel

Wheels turn around an axle. They are used to move things smoothly.

Slope

We use slopes in many machines. Rolling something up a slope is often easier than lifting it straight up in the air.

Pulley

A pulley uses a wheel and a rope to lift very heavy loads.

Pulley

Cranes use pulleys to raise and lower loads.

Find out more Bicycles 29   Science 122

Magnets

Magnet uses

Fridge magnets are used to hold notes on a fridge.

Metal detectors use magnets to find metal objects under the ground.

Magnets are used in spacecraft to stop things from floating around.

Phones and many other electrical machines use magnets.

Magnets are made from iron or steel. They look like ordinary metal, but have the power to pull things toward or push things away from them.

Magnetic poles
The two ends of a magnet are called the north and south poles.

Around each pole is a magnetic field.

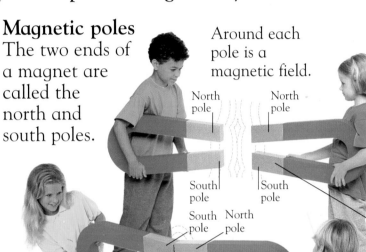

North pole

North pole

South pole

South pole

South pole

North pole

North pole

South pole

Magnetic forces pull two different poles together.

Man-made magnet

Natural magnet
Lodestone is a natural magnetic rock. Most magnets are man-made.

Lodestone

The magnetic field is a powerful, invisible magnetic force.

Magnetic forces push the same poles apart.

Magnetic materials
Magnets only attract certain kinds of metals, such as iron and steel.

Steel spoon

Iron nails

Steel paper clips

Magnetic Earth
The biggest magnet of all is the Earth. It has two magnetic poles that create a magnetic force around Earth.

Magnetic north pole

Magnetic south pole

Compass
Compass needles always point to the magnetic north pole.

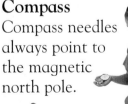

Compass

A **ship's compass** helps sailors find their way.

Northern lights
This light show in the sky is created by the magnetic force around the Earth.

Find out more ➤ North America 102   Pirates 108

World of Nature

Mammals

Many of the animals we know best are mammals. Cats, cows, monkeys, and mice are all mammals. So are human beings.

Large eyes see well, even in the dark.

Long whiskers touch and feel.

Sharp teeth catch and chew food.

Leopard
The different parts of a leopard's body help it survive. Other land mammals have similar kinds of bodies.

Did you know?
The biggest mammal in the world is the blue whale. It is as heavy as 2,000 people!

Marsupial mammals
Some mammals, like this kangaroo, have furry pouches on their tummies. Their babies spend months inside growing.

Long tail for balance

Strong claws help in climbing trees.

Dappled fur for camouflage among the trees

Mammal facts

Echidna

Mammals have fur, hair, or even spines on their bodies.

Wolf

Mammals are warm to the touch. They need food for energy.

Chimp

Mammals have larger brains than other animals.

Mammal babies feed on their mother's milk.

Mother and baby
Baby mammals grow inside their mother's body until they are born.

Newborn puppy

Baby puppies grow bigger on their mother's milk.

Playing and fighting together makes the puppies grow stronger.

Giraffes

Find out more ⟩ ★ Animals 17 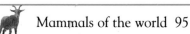 Mammals of the world 95

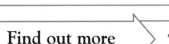

World of Nature

Mammals of the world

There are only about 4,000 different kinds of mammals, but they live in every part of the world – on land, in the sea, and in the air.

Reindeer
Reindeer live in snowy northern wastelands. Some are kept for meat and leather.

Bat
Bats are the only mammals that can fly. They live in large groups in caves all over the world.

Bush baby
Bush babies have huge eyes. They hunt at night among the trees of African rain forests.

Otter
Otters are expert divers and live and feed in the rivers of North America.

Dolphin
Dolphins are found in all the oceans of the world. They live in large groups called herds.

Porcupine
Porcupines live in North America. They raise their sharp quills to protect themselves.

ARCTIC OCEAN

NORTH AMERICA

EUROPE

ASIA

PACIFIC OCEAN

AFRICA

SOUTH AMERICA

ATLANTIC OCEAN

INDIAN OCEAN

AUSTRALASIA

ANTARCTICA

Mouse
Mice are found all over the world. They often live in people's homes, eating crumbs.

Brown bear
The European bear climbs trees to raid bees' nests for their honey.

Mountain goat
These goats are very surefooted. They live on mountain slopes in North America.

Zebra
Zebras live on the grassy plains of Africa. Their stripes help camouflage them in a group.

Did you know?
When they are attacked, skunks spray a horrible-smelling liquid at their enemy, then run away.

Rhinoceros
Rhinos are found in Africa and Asia. They use their fierce-looking horns to defend themselves.

Life Today

Maps

World map

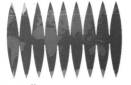

1 A globe is the most accurate map of the world.

2 A flat map is made by flattening out the globe.

3 The gaps are filled in with extra bits of land and ocean.

Did you know?
Space satellites take photos of the Earth to help people make more accurate maps.

Map reading
You must be able to read a map to find your way.

Symbols
The special signs on a map are symbols. A symbol represents something real. Symbols are explained in a key.

Key

 A very beautiful place

 A good viewpoint

 Tourist information

Maps are pictures that show places, such as towns, from above. We use maps to find our way around.

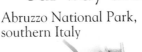

Abruzzo National Park, southern Italy

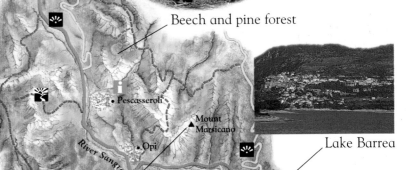

Beech and pine forest

Pescasseroli

Mount Marsicano

River Sangro

Opi

River Melfa

Lake Barrea

Mount Marsicano

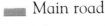

Main road

Minor road

- - - Footpath

A **compass** always points to the north. It helps you find your way with a map.

Lake Barrea

N

This symbol shows you where north is on the map.

Types of maps

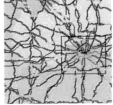

Street maps name all the streets in a town or city.

Weather maps show the weather in different places.

Subway maps show where underground train lines go.

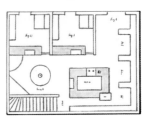

Floor plans show you the layout of a building.

Road maps help drivers plan a journey.

Find out more Explorers 61 Magnets 93

Science and Technology

Materials

Steel is strong, glass is clear, cotton is soft – every material has special qualities. Everything we use is made from materials just right for the job.

Cotton
Some materials, such as cotton, are found naturally. Others are made in factories.

Cotton plant

Cotton is turned into thread to make clothes.

Materials for different jobs

Aluminum foil can withstand high temperatures. It is used for cooking.

Natural sponges soak up lots of water. They are good for washing with.

Polyester fabric is made in factories. It is soft and often used to make teddy bears.

Glass
Glass is useful because you can see through it. It is made from sand, limestone, and soda.

Steel
Steel is a hard, strong metal. It is made from limestone, carbon, and iron melted down together.

Plastic
Plastic is strong and does not rot or rust. It is made from heated oil.

Wood is naturally hard and strong. It is often used to make furniture.

New materials
New artificial materials are being invented all the time.

Lycra clothes fit comfortably.

Bullet proof vest made of Kevlar

Recycling
Some materials, like glass, can be recycled to make new products.

Recycled glass

Find out more   Conservation 43   North America: culture 105

Science and Technology

Moon

Moon machines

This **Moon buggy** is used by astronauts to move around the Moon quickly.

This **lunokhod** is a Russian vehicle. It was put on the Moon to take photographs.

A **lunar module** carried astronauts from their spacecraft to the Moon surface.

The Moon is a ball of rock that circles the Earth. It is our nearest neighbor in space. Astronauts have landed on and mapped its surface.

Moon surface
There are flat plains, valleys, mountains, and craters on the Moon's surface.

Astronaut

Dusty surface

Low land filled in by the lava of ancient volcanoes

Bare rocks

Moon from Earth
The Moon looks bright because one side is lit by the Sun.

Did you know?
It's possible to jump six times higher on the Moon than on Earth thanks to the weaker gravity there!

Climate
Because there is no wind or rain on the Moon, flags won't fly and footprints will never disappear.

Astronaut's footprint

American flag is held up by wire.

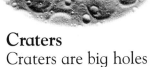

Craters
Craters are big holes on the Moon's surface.

Moon phases
As the Moon travels around the Earth, we see different parts of its sunlit side. This gives us the phases of the Moon.

Full Moon

Crescent Moon

Half Moon

Find out more Planets 109    Space travel 133

Mountains

The high, rocky slopes of mountains are battered by cold winds and covered by heavy snow. They make a harsh habitat for animals and plants.

Lichen
Lichens grow high up because they can survive extreme cold.

Mountain animals

Mountain plants
To survive the harsh conditions, mountain plants have special shapes and parts.

Trees cannot grow above the tree line.

Coniferous forests grow on the higher slopes.

Vultures' large wings allow them to glide on strong mountain winds.

Poor, thin soil

A **bobcat's** spotted coat helps it blend in with its rocky mountain home.

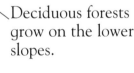

Deciduous forests grow on the lower slopes.

Rhododendron
Thick, shiny leaves save this plant from the cold.

Bell heather
The tiny leaves of this heather can withstand strong winds.

Rock rose
Rock roses grow close to the ground to stay out of the wind.

Chinchillas have thick fur coats to protect them from the cold.

Did you know?
In 1963, a volcanic island suddenly appeared in the sea. Called Surtsey, it is now home to plants.

Volcano
When volcanoes erupt, they shoot out molten rock. This can build a mountain in less than a week!

Mountain goats have specially shaped hooves to help them clamber over rocks.

Find out more   Asia 20   Plants 110

Life Today

Music

Types of music

Popular music is fun and catchy. It is often good for dancing.

Nursery rhymes are simple songs for young children.

Choral music is usually religious. It is sung by groups called choirs.

Classical music is written by composers for instruments in an orchestra.

Music in the home
Most people listen to recorded music at home.

Compact disc   Personal stereo

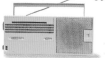

Radio

Music is a pattern of sounds made by musical instruments and human voices. People enjoy different kinds of music all over the world.

African music
African music is based on strong rhythms – perfect for dancing to.

Wooden drums beat out the rhythm.

Musical notes
Music is written on a set of lines, using notes instead of words.

Dancing to the beat

Indian music
Indian music has a haunting sound. It is often played on a sitar.

Moroccan music
Moroccan music is often based around folk stories and dance.

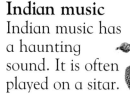

Mexican music
Mexican bands play traditional folk music on violins and guitars.

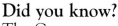

Did you know?
The German composer Beethoven was only three when he performed his first piece of music!

Find out more Festivals 65   Musical instruments 101

Musical instruments

Most instruments belong to one of five groups. Each group makes musical sounds in a different way.

A **double bass** is one of the largest instruments. It has a very deep sound.

Sitars are Indian stringed instruments.

Bow scrapes strings.

Four strings

Wooden body

Metal spike to rest on

String instruments
These instruments can be strummed, plucked, or bowed.

Chamber group
Stringed instruments are often played in small groups.

Percussion
These instruments make a sound when they are hit or shaken.

Maracas are rattles. They make a swishing sound.

Tambourines have jingling metal disks.

Triangles make a clear, tinkling sound.

Electronic instruments
These use electricity to make sounds.

Electric keyboards can make the sounds of many different instruments.

Electric drums can only be heard through loudspeakers.

Woodwind
Woodwind instruments make a sound when you blow air inside them.

Recorders are one of the simplest woodwind instruments.

Flutes are made of metal.

Oboes have keys for fingers. The mouthpiece is made from a reed.

Accordions blow air with bellows to make sound.

Brass
Musicians blow and vibrate their lips to make brass instruments sound.

French horns have long pipes that end in a large bell.

Digeridoos are made from a hollow branch.

Trumpets have a narrow tube bent around twice. The valves control the tone.

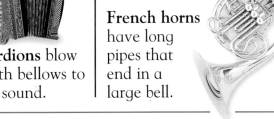

Find out more   Sound 129   Theater 139

North America

Canada and Alaska

North America reaches as far north as the Arctic Ocean. Its rivers, peaks, forests, and lakes are a haven for wildlife.

Continents of the World

Did you know?
- Canada is the second biggest country in the world.
- Greenland is the world's largest island.

Tundra
In the far north is a frozen, treeless plain called the tundra.

Greenland
Greenland lies in the Arctic Ocean. Much of the land is covered in ice.

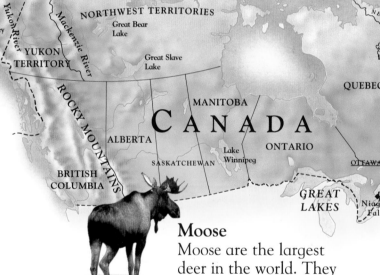

ALASKA (US)
Mount McKinley (Denali)
Yukon River
Mackenzie River
YUKON TERRITORY
NORTHWEST TERRITORIES
Great Bear Lake
Great Slave Lake
Queen Elizabeth Islands
Baffin Island
GREENLAND (DENMARK)
NEWFOUNDLAND
Smallwood Reservoir
QUEBEC
St. Lawrence River
PRINCE EDWARD ISLAND
NOVA SCOTIA
NEW BRUNSWICK
ROCKY MOUNTAINS
ALBERTA
BRITISH COLUMBIA
SASKATCHEWAN
MANITOBA
CANADA
Lake Winnipeg
ONTARIO
OTTAWA
GREAT LAKES
Niagara Falls

Glacier
Alaska has huge rivers of ice called glaciers.

Northern lights
These glowing lights can be seen in the skies above Canada.

Mount McKinley
Mount McKinley in Alaska is the US's highest peak.

Moose
Moose are the largest deer in the world. They feed only on plants.

Grizzly bear
Grizzly bears live in the Rocky Mountains. They feed on animals and plants.

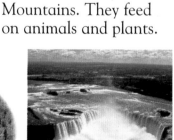

Pine forests
Forests cover more than one-third of Canada. Many animals shelter here.

Niagara Falls
The Niagara Falls in Canada are made up of two thundering waterfalls.

Find out more ➤ Forests 73   Magnets 93

Continents of the World

North America: culture

Canada and Alaska
This huge landmass has a small population. Most of the people live in cities in the warmer south.

Fishing
Fishing in Canada's lakes and oceans is a popular sport and an important industry.

Culture

The **maple leaf** is the national emblem of Canada.

Ice hockey is a popular winter sport, and is followed by many fans.

Native Americans were the first people to live in Canada.

Forestry, Canada
Forestry is one of Canada's most important industries. The pine trees are made into timber and paper.

Truck carries logs to sawmill.

Felled trees

Many **French-speaking Canadians** live in the province of Quebec.

Farming
Canada's farmers raise cattle or grow huge fields of wheat on the prairies.

Rodeos celebrate the skills and courage of cowboys.

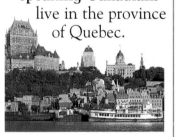

Industry

Mining is important. Most of the world's zinc and nickel is mined here.

Zinc   Nickel

Oil is drilled in Alaska. It is then transported south along the world's longest pipeline.

Continents of the World

North America

US and Mexico

With mountains in the west and east and deserts in the south, North America has some spectacular scenery.

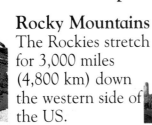

Rocky Mountains
The Rockies stretch for 3,000 miles (4,800 km) down the western side of the US.

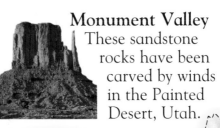

Monument Valley
These sandstone rocks have been carved by winds in the Painted Desert, Utah.

Great Lakes
The five Great Lakes make up the largest area of freshwater in the world.

States
1 VERMONT
2 NEW JERSEY
3 DELAWARE
4 MARYLAND
5 CONNECTICUT
6 NEW HAMPSHIRE
7 MASSACHUSETTS
8 RHODE ISLAND

Everglades
This vast tropical marsh in Florida is home to animals such as alligators.

Collared lizard
This lizard manages to survive in the dry deserts.

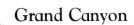

Grand Canyon
This deep, rocky gorge has been cut out in Arizona by the Colorado River.

Death Valley
Death Valley in California is the hottest, driest place in the whole of North America.

Sonoran Desert
This desert lies between the US and Mexico. It is famous for its giant cacti.

Okefenokee Swamp
This freshwater swamp in southern Georgia is a safe refuge for wildlife.

Continents of the World

North America: culture

US and Mexico
The US and Mexico are large, modern countries. But they both have strong traditions and cultures.

New York
This is the largest city in the US and is the country's business center.

Silicon valley   Silicon chip

Chrysler building

Industry
The US's famous computer industry is in Silicon Valley, California.

Farming
The prairies in central America are very fertile. They are used to grow wheat and other cereals.

Culture

Baseball is the national sport of the US.

Hollywood in Los Angeles is the film capital of the world.

Rock and roll was invented in the US.

Jazz music began in the southern states of America.

Ancient ruins

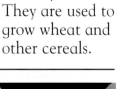

Ancient temples were built in Mexico many hundreds of years ago.

Traditional crafts
Many traditional goods are still made throughout the US and Mexico.

Mexican masks   American quilt   Navajo rug

Tourism
Millions of people visit North America every year to see its famous landmarks and scenery.

Florida

White House

Las Vegas

Find out more Grasslands 77   Incas 85

Science and Technology

Oil

Fuels from oil
Different parts of the crude oil are used to make other fuels.

Propane gas can be stored in bottles and tanks and used for cooking and heating.

Paraffin oil is used in lamps and heaters. It is also mixed into paint to make it smooth.

Oil is used as a lubricant. It helps machine parts slide against each other.

Gasoline is one of the most important products of oil. It is a fuel for cars.

Oil is formed over millions of years. It is found deep inside the Earth, and is pumped out to make many different kinds of fuel.

Oil rig
Drills on an oil rig dig deep into the seabed for oil and gas, which is then pumped up and taken to the shore via pipes.

Crude oil
Crude oil is the thick, dark liquid that comes out of the ground.

Nodding donkey
This is a small oil rig that pumps up oil found under land.

Gases are burned off.

Crane lifts heavy drill parts

Workers live on an oil rig for weeks at a time.

The oil rig's concrete legs rest on the sea bed.

Drilling
Holes called wells are drilled deep underground to collect the oil.

Drill bit
The bits have strong steel teeth to cut into hard ground.

Oil refinery
Crude oil is taken to a refinery. Here it is heated until it separates into different parts.

Heating towers

Waste gases are burned off.

Did you know?
Drill bits get so worn down by the hard rock that they need replacing twice a day.

Painting

Life Today

Types of paintings

A **self-portrait** is an artist's painting of him- or herself.

Murals are large paintings that are done on a wall.

Portraits are pictures of people. They are not always true to life!

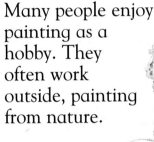

Abstract paintings use lines, shapes, and colors.

Landscapes are paintings of outdoor scenes.

People have painted pictures for thousands of years, creating works of art on walls, wood, paper, or canvas.

Painter at work

Many people enjoy painting as a hobby. They often work outside, painting from nature.

Easel for supporting the picture

Paints

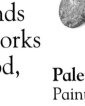

Palette
Painters mix oil paints on a special wooden palette.

Did you know?
In the past, black paint was sometimes made out of ground-up mummies!

Painting surfaces

Artists paint on different surfaces, such as paper or canvas.

Paper   Canvas

Picture frames

A picture frame helps display a painting and protects it as it hangs on a wall.

Paints and inks

Artists create pictures with various materials. This makes their works look very different.

Pen-and-ink drawing

Oil painting

Watercolor painting

Life in the Past

Pirates

Pirate ships
Pirate ships were small and fast. They were only recognizable by their unusual flag!

Navigation
Pirates used the Sun, stars, instruments, and maps to find their way at sea.

Pirates were the robbers of the seas. They attacked ships and stole their cargo, and sometimes even the ship itself!

Figurehead
Sailors believed that a figurehead on the boat would protect them.

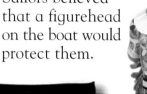

The Jolly Roger – the pirates' flag

Death's skull

Crossed swords

Map

Telescope

Compass

Pirate attack
Pirates attacked ships and then pulled them close with iron hooks.

Cannon

Iron hook

Pirate's life
Many pirates led awful lives. At sea, they ate hard biscuits and limes to stay healthy.

Limes   Biscuits

Punishment
If pirates were caught, they were hanged. Their bodies were hung in an iron cage to warn others.

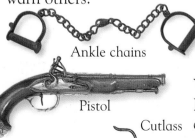

Ankle chains

Iron cage

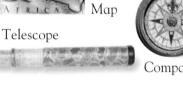

Handcuffs

Weapons
Every pirate was armed with a pistol and a short, sharp sword called a cutlass.

Pistol

Cutlass

Treasure chest

Treasure
Pirates attacked merchant ships to steal their valuable cargo. They shared out the lost treasure between them.

Silver coins   Rings

Did you know?
When the pirate Blackbeard went into battle, he set fire to string in his hair!

Diamond and amethyst necklace

 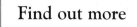

Science and Technology

Planets

Planets are huge balls of rock, metal, and gas that travel around a star in space. The Earth is one of a family of nine planets that circle the Sun.

Mercury
Mercury is closest to the Sun. It's boiling hot by day and freezing cold at night.

Cold surface

Jupiter
Jupiter is the biggest planet. It is made up of hot, runny rock and swirling gases.

Jupiter is larger than all the other planets put together.

A red spot is a great storm.

Saturn
Saturn's shining rings are made up of ice, rocks, and dust.

Venus
Venus is the hottest planet. It is covered in thick clouds of gas.

Asteroids and meteorites
These are tiny planets made up of rocks and metal.

Earth
Earth is the only planet with air and water, vital to all living things.

Mars
Mars is very cold, and covered in dead volcanoes, craters, and dusty red soil.

Asteroids are larger than meteorites.

Pluto
Pluto is the smallest planet. It lies farthest from the Sun.

Neptune
Neptune has cold winds that blow as fast as the Concorde.

Uranus
Uranus is covered with a thick layer of beautiful blue-green gas.

Meteorite fragments

Solar System
Four planets lie close to the Sun. Five planets lie much farther away.

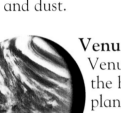

Sun Venus
Earth
Mercury Mars Jupiter Saturn Uranus Neptune Pluto

Find out more Moon 98   Sun and stars 137

Plants

Types of plants

Cacti grow in hot, dry areas and store water in their stems.

Mosses grow in moist soils. They never flower.

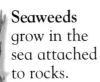

Seaweeds grow in the sea attached to rocks.

Grasses are an important food for many animals.

Trees are the biggest plants. Their trunks are really very large stems.

There are more than 425,000 different plants in the world, and they come in every shape and size – from delicate seaweeds to towering trees.

Flowers make seeds.

Shrub
All plants have the same basic parts, just like this *Skimmia* shrub.

Leaves make food for the whole plant.

Food
Plants use air, water, the green in their leaves – chlorophyll, and the sun's energy to make food.

Stems carry water and food to the whole plant.

Roots take up water from the soil and hold the plant in the ground.

First leaves open.

Seed leaves wither.

Sprouting seed

Beechnut seeds

1 The seed soaks up water, swells, and splits.

2 A tiny root grows down into the soil.

Seed case

3 A shoot grows up toward the light.

Did you know?
Giant kelp seaweed grows so tall it would reach higher than the Leaning Tower of Pisa in Italy!

Plants as food

Corn is made up of seeds.

Tarragon is a leaf.   **A carrot** is a root.

Cabbage is a group of leaves.

Broccoli is a mix of flowers and stems!

Ginger is a root.   **A tomato** is a fruit.

Find out more Flowers 69   Fruits and seeds 75

World of Nature

Polar animals

Around the north and south poles it is bitterly cold and windy. But many animals have found different ways to survive here.

Migration

Reindeer migrate south from the Arctic in winter to find food and shelter.

Seal
Weddel seals spend winter under the Antarctic ice sheet. They breathe through holes in the ice.

Flippers push the penguin through water.

Beak has feathers for warmth

Snowy owls also travel south in winter. They feed on Arctic rabbits.

Penguin
Emperor penguins live on the Antarctic ice, huddling together in groups to keep warm. They can't fly, but are expert swimmers.

Wolf
Wolves have hairs under their paws to give them a good grip on ice.

Musk oxen move south from the Arctic in the winter to find grazing land.

Closely packed feathers

Polar bear
Polar bears have thick, oily coats to keep out the cold. They are the only mammal to live on the Arctic ice.

Feet are small to cut down heat loss.

Krill
Krill are tiny shrimp-like animals that live in the seas around Antarctica.

Walrus
A thick layer of fatty blubber keeps the walrus warm in cold Arctic seas.

Moose travel north to the Arctic shore in the summer to escape all the flies in the south.

Find out more Seasons 126   Polar lands 112

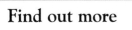

World of Nature

Polar lands

The polar lands lie around the north and south poles. The frozen ground and icy climate make them a hard place for plants to grow.

Antarctica
No one lives in the Antarctic, but scientists visit to study the land and its wildlife.

Polar plants

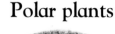

Mosses grow in thick cushions. This protects them from icy winds.

The **Arctic wormwood** stores food in its roots to help it survive.

Ice field
A lot of the land in the polar regions is covered by huge sheets of ice, called ice fields.

Glaciers flow from the ice fields.

Glaciers are rivers of ice that move slowly down mountain slopes.

Grasses grow quickly in the spring when there are long periods of daylight.

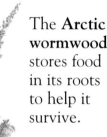

Primroses have long roots to help them survive.

Tundra
The tundra is the frozen land in the far north. The ice melts here in the summer, and a few plants manage to grow.

Life in the Arctic
People have lived in the Arctic for thousands of years. They have had to adapt their lifestyle to the harsh climate.

Did you know?
The tallest ever iceberg was higher than St. Paul's Cathedral, London.

Winter coat

Dog-pulled sleds make it possible to move goods across the ice.

Warm clothes are made from animal skins.

Husky

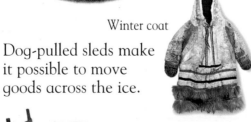

Sled

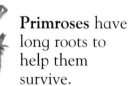

Fleabane grows only for a few weeks in the Arctic summer.

Find out more   Antarctica 19   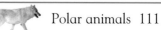 Polar animals 111

World of Nature

Rain forest animals

Flying animals

Morpho butterflies have bright colors to help them attract a mate.

Scarlet macaws have hooked beaks that can crack open nuts.

Toucans use their long beaks to pick fruit and steal other birds' eggs.

Fruit bats rest during the day in the forest canopy.

Monkeys howl, parrots shriek, and insects chirp – tropical rain forests are noisy places, home to a huge variety of wildlife.

Spider monkey
Monkeys swing through the canopy, gripping the branches with their strong feet, hands, and tails.

Tree snake
These snakes live in trees near water. They eat frogs and lizards.

Thick, woolly coat

The monkey's tail can support it from a branch.

Baby monkey clings to its mother.

Monkeys feed on tasty fruit and leaves.

Jaguar
The jaguar's coat helps hide it in the dappled forest light.

Did you know?
Scarlet macaws can tell each other apart by special patterns on their feathers.

Tree frogs
Tree frogs spend their lives high up in tree branches.

Three-toed sloth
Sloths have hooklike claws that cling on to branches.

Gecko
The gecko's clever camouflage hides it from hungry snakes.

Ants
These ants eat a fungus that grows on the leaves they cut and store.

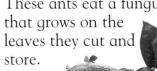

Find out more > Rain forests 114   South America 131

113

World of Nature

Rain forests

Forest flowers

Slipper orchids are pollinated by only one type of bee.

Shaving brush trees attract bats with their scented flowers.

Steriphomas flowers are tube-shaped. Only long-tongued insects can feed on them.

The **hotlips plant** has beautiful bright red flowers.

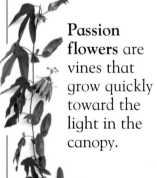

Passion flowers are vines that grow quickly toward the light in the canopy.

Tropical rain forests are hot, sticky places packed with trees and vines. All the plants and daily rainfall make them dark and steamy.

Trees grow tall to reach the sun.

The forest roof, about 130 ft (40 m) above the ground, is called the canopy.

Thick leaves and branches

Leaves stay on the trees all year round.

Vines climb up trees.

Young sapling

Did you know?
There are many plants and animals in the rain forests that have not yet been discovered by people.

Rain forest layers
A rain forest is like a tall building with many levels. Different plants grow to different heights.

Only smaller tree varieties grow lower down, where it is shady.

Forest floor is dark and wet

Rain forest tribes
The Txucuhamai tribe has lived in South American rain forests for thousands of years.

Forest fruit
Rain forest plants provide us with all sorts of delicious foods to eat.

Bread fruit   Nutmeg

Cocoa   Ginger   Pineapple

Find out more Animals in danger 18   Conservation 43

Life Today

Religion

The Bible is the Christian holy book.

There are five main world religions. Christians, Jews, and Muslims believe in one god, Hindus believe in many, and Buddhists do not worship a god.

Christianity
Christians worship one god. They believe that God's son, Jesus Christ, lived on Earth about 2,000 years ago.

The Christian symbol is a cross.

Angels

Mary, mother of Jesus

Judaism
Judaism was the first religion to believe in one god, about 4,000 years ago. Its followers are called Jews.

Men wear skullcaps.

Candles for a Jewish festival

The Torah is the holy book.

A shrine, for prayers at home

Hinduism
Hinduism is an Asian religion. The followers called Hindus, worship many gods.

Snake mask to chase off evil

The Hindu God Shiva

Sacred words on an Islamic tile

Some muslims pray on a mat.

The Koran is the Muslim holy book.

Islam
The religion of Islam began with the prophet Muhammed. Followers of Islam are called Muslims. They worship one god.

Buddhism
Buddhism began in India. Its followers are called Buddhists and believe that they will be born again after they die.

The Buddhist wheel of life

Prayer wheel

The Buddha was a prince who became a monk.

Places of worship
Each religion has special buildings in which people get together to pray. They are guided by a religious leader.

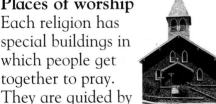
Christian church

Muslim mosque

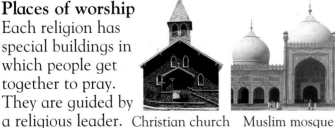
Buddhist temple

Hindu temple

Jewish synagogue

Find out more 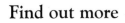 Books 32 Buildings 35

Reptiles

World of Nature

Lizards, tortoises, crocodiles, and snakes are all reptiles. Most of them live in warm places, have dry, scaly skin, and lay eggs on dry land.

Reptile families

Sinaloan milk snake

Snakes are expert hunters. They poison their prey or squeeze it to death.

Alligator snapping turtle

Turtles are excellent swimmers. They only come on land to lay their eggs.

Basilisk lizard

Lizards make up over half of all reptiles. They are small, quick, and feed on insects.

Hermann's tortoise

Tortoises live on land. Their hard shells protect them from their enemies.

The scales are like armor for protection.

Strong tail for swimming

Reptile eggs
Baby snakes cut their way out of their shell with a special tiny egg tooth.

Rat snake

Eye

Long, snapping jaws and sharp teeth catch prey.

Webbed feet move like paddles.

Did you know?
Many snakes eat their food while it is still alive!

Crocodile
Crocodiles live and catch their food in rivers. Their bodies are perfect for hunting in water.

Baby caiman

Baby reptiles
Unlike most reptiles, crocodiles take care of their babies for a few weeks after hatching.

Cold blooded
Reptiles are cold blooded. They need heat from the sun to warm up and shady places to cool down.

Garden lizard

Lizard tails
If a lizard's tail is grabbed by an enemy, it can break off, letting the lizard escape. A new tail soon grows back.

Tree skink

Broken tail

Newly grown tail

Find out more Animals 17 Reptiles of the world 117

Reptiles of the world

Alligator
Alligators live in the swamps of the south eastern US. When resting, they open their mouths to cool down.

There are more than 6,000 different kinds of reptiles, and most of them live where it is warm. Some live in water, but many more prefer to stay on dry land.

European grass snake
To escape its enemies, this snake lies upside down and pretends to be dead.

Soft-shelled turtle
This turtle lives in North America. It is usually found buried in mud in rivers and ponds.

Cobra
This cobra has a poisonous bite that can kill in minutes. It lives in Asia.

Tegu lizard
This South American lizard has a tough skin made from horny scales.

Pricklenape agama
The agama lives in northern African deserts. When food is scarce, it survives on fat in its tail.

Crested water dragon
This lizard lives in Asia and can run faster on two legs than it can on four.

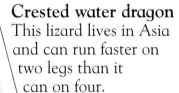

Did you know?
When it's attacked, a horned toad squirts blood from its eyes to shock its enemies.

Chameleon
Chameleons live in African rain forests. They can use their amazing eyes to look in two directions at once!

Frilled lizard
Found in the dry bushlands of Australia, this lizard puts up its frill to frighten off enemies.

Find out more Desert animals 45 Reptiles 116

River animals

World of Nature

Flying visitors

Bats swoop over rivers at night to catch small flying insects.

Kingfishers catch fish by diving headfirst into rivers.

Herons stand in the water waiting to stab fish and eels with their sharp beaks.

All kinds of animals live in or near the world's rivers. Strong swimmers live in fast-flowing rivers, but most animals choose quieter streams.

Water rat
Water rats make their homes in riverbanks.

Mayfly
Mayfly young are called larvae and live underwater. The adults fly in the air above.

Beaver
Beavers build dams across small rivers. They use trees they have felled with their sharp teeth.

The lodge is built with logs above the water level.

A beaver's home is called a lodge.

Did you know?
Water beetles breathe underwater by trapping an air bubble under their wings.

Water snake
Water snakes have thick, scaly skins to keep out water.

River

Dam

Leeches
Leeches cling to stones on riverbeds, so they won't be swept away.

River shellfish
These shellfish live in fast-flowing water. They feed on water plants.

Trout
Trout live in swift, shallow streams. The females lay their eggs in the riverbed.

Crayfish
Crayfish live in fast-flowing rivers, feeding on small fish and worms.

Find out more Animal homes 16   Rivers and lakes 119

Rivers and lakes

Rivers are always on the move. They carry rainwater downhill, from mountains to the ocean.

Uses of rivers and lakes

Water sports, such as fishing and sailing, are popular activities.

1 River source
Rainwater trickles into the ground. It comes out at one place – a river's source.

2 Stream
From the source, a small stream flows downhill. The water is clean and fast flowing.

A river's course
Rivers start life as trickles, but as they flow into each other, they become larger and slower.

Shallow stream

Fast-flowing water

Big rocks

Clear, clean water

Hydroelectric power stations make electricity from the power of a river.

Water transportation is an important way of moving goods from place to place.

3 River
A stream becomes a river as more water flows in. It forms big bends called meanders.

4 River mouth
The river flows into the ocean. This is called the river mouth.

Lakes
Lakes are dips in the ground that are filled by rain- and river water. Some lakes are man-made.

Reservoirs are built by people.

Crater lakes form naturally when rainwater collects inside a volcano.

Irrigation pumps water from lakes and rivers to dry fields to help crops grow.

Find out more ▶ River animals 118   Water 146

Science and Technology

Rocks and minerals

Minerals
Rocks are made of tiny grains called minerals. Some minerals form beautiful stones.

Opals are valued for their beauty.

Diamonds are the hardest of all minerals.

Jade is very hard. It is often used for carving.

Gold is a precious metal. It, too, is formed by minerals.

Copper pipe

Copper is an ore mineral. Most useful metals come from ore minerals.

Pencil

Graphite is one of the softest minerals. It is used in pencils.

The world around us is made of rock. We use rocks and minerals for many things, from buildings to jewelry.

Rock types
There are three main types of rocks. They are formed in different ways.

Sedimentary rock
Sedimentary rock is made from layers of mud, sand, and stones that have been squashed together.

Conglomerate rock

Metamorphic rock
Metamorphic rocks are sedimentary or igneous rocks that have been changed by great heat, great pressure, or both.

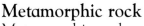

Marble

Did you know?
The largest diamond in the world is called the Cullinand. It is as heavy as a pineapple.

Granite

Igneous rock
Igneous rock is made from hot, runny rock deep inside the Earth that has cooled and hardened.

Using rocks and minerals

Chalk is a soft sedimentary rock used for writing.

Chalkboards are made from a metamorphic rock called slate.

12345 678910

Paint can be made from colored minerals in rocks.

Azurite blue paint

Vermilion paint

Sculptures are often cut from igneous rocks, such as marble.

Tin cans used to be made from tin ore.

Find out more ▶ Earth 50   Early humans 49

Romans

Life in the Past

The Romans were a powerful people who lived in Europe about 2,000 years ago. They ruled over a huge empire.

Roman life

Baths were places to relax and wash. They were built in every town.

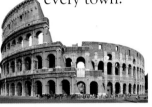

Amphitheaters were huge stadiums. Many public sports were played here.

Temples were fine stone buildings that the Romans built to worship their gods.

Fountains provided townspeople with fresh drinking water.

Roman soldier
The Roman army was one of the best in the world. Its soldiers were expertly trained and well armed.

Javelin

Armor of metal strips

Roman road
The Romans were great builders. Their roads and aqueducts were strong.

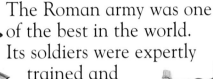

Backpack
A soldier carried a bag, tool kit, and pots and pans.

Weapons
In battle, soldiers fought with spears, swords, and daggers.

Woolen tunic

Sandals
A soldier's sandals were studded with nails so they'd last.

Belt
Every soldier wore a belt of leather and metal.

Shield

Emperor
For more than 400 years, the Romans were ruled by emperors.

Coins stamped with emperor's portrait

Emperors wore a crown of leaves.

Augustus

Did you know?
Roman men wore robes called togas. Pants were thought to be unmanly!

Science

Types of scientists

Chemists produce new foods, drugs, and materials.

Radiologists take X rays and study the results.

Forensic scientists study the clues that can solve crimes.

Zoologists study animals and how they live.

Geologists study rocks to find out about the Earth.

Science is observing, examining, and learning about the world around us. Scientists often find new ways to improve people's lives.

Laboratory
Many scientists work in laboratories. These rooms have the special equipment scientists need to perform and record experiment results.

Did you know?
Isaac Newton figured out the laws of gravity when an apple fell on his head.

Bunsen burner

Chemical solutions

Scientist

Test tubes

Flask

Microscope

Experimenting
Scientists learn by doing experiments.

1 Scientists ask a question and come up with a possible solution.

2 They do tests to prove they are right.

3 They take measurements and keep careful records as proof.

Find out more Air 9   Hospitals and doctors 79

Sea animals

Salty seawater covers nearly three-quarters of the Earth's surface. Below the waves, the oceans teem with a huge variety of sea life.

Did you know?
Flying fish can leap from the water, spread out their fins, and glide through the air.

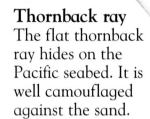

Thornback ray
The flat thornback ray hides on the Pacific seabed. It is well camouflaged against the sand.

Narwhal
The narwhal whale has a twisted tusk and lives in the icy waters of the Arctic Ocean.

Starfish
Starfish cling to the rocky seashores of the Atlantic Ocean. They use their arms to pry open seashells.

Deep-sea hatchet
Named after its big, axlike belly, this hatchet lives in the deep waters of the Pacific Ocean.

ARCTIC OCEAN
EUROPE
NORTH AMERICA
ASIA
PACIFIC
ATLANTIC OCEAN
AFRICA
INDIAN OCEAN
SOUTH AMERICA
OCEAN
AUSTRALASIA
ANTARCTICA

Dugong
Dugongs are gentle mammals that swim in large herds in the shallow waters of the Pacific.

Zooplankton
Billions of tiny sea creatures called zooplankton float in all the world's oceans.

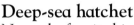

Octopus
This octopus inhabits the warm coastal waters of the Atlantic. It wraps its prey up in its tentacles.

Sea horse
Sea horses are the only fish that swim upright. They are found among the coral reefs off Africa.

Sperm whale
Huge sperm whales eat tons of plankton a day. They live in the Atlantic and Pacific oceans.

World of Nature

Seas and oceans

From space, the Earth looks blue because most of it is covered by water. Below the waves is a secret world we are only just beginning to explore.

Did you know?
At its deepest point, the Marianas Trench stretches down 7 miles (11 km).

The world's oceans
There are four main oceans in the world. They cover nearly three-quarters of the Earth's surface.

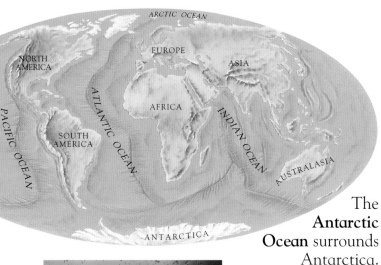

ARCTIC OCEAN

NORTH AMERICA

EUROPE

ASIA

ATLANTIC OCEAN

AFRICA

PACIFIC OCEAN

SOUTH AMERICA

INDIAN OCEAN

AUSTRALASIA

ANTARCTICA

The **Arctic Ocean** is the smallest ocean. It freezes over in the winter months, and only icebreaker ships can get through.

The **Antarctic Ocean** surrounds Antarctica.

The **Indian Ocean** stretches between Africa and Australia. Coral reefs grow in the warm, shallow waters close to shore.

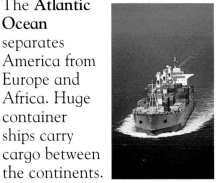

The **Pacific Ocean** is bigger than all the other oceans put together. It has huge waves.

The **Atlantic Ocean** separates America from Europe and Africa. Huge container ships carry cargo between the continents.

Sea exploration

Canoes were used by the first explorers. Wind and sea currents helped them move.

Spanish sailing ship

Sailing ships were used by explorers 500 years ago to sail around the world.

Submarines are used by today's explorers to study the seabed under the ocean.

The seabed
If you drained away the oceans, you'd see the seabed has valleys and mountains just like dry land.

Land   Continental shelf
Slope   Underwater mountain
Deep-ocean floor
Ocean trench

Find out more Fish of the world 68   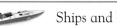 Ships and boats 127

World of Nature

Seashore

The seashore, where the sea meets the land, is home to a huge variety of plants and animals. They have all had to adapt to saltwater, strong winds, and waves.

Did you know?
This crab holds a sea anemone in each of its pincers. If a fish attacks, the sea anemone stings it!

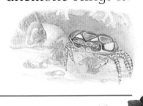

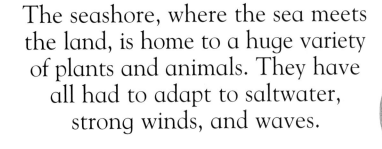

Seaweed · Sea anemones · Winkle · Limpet

Crab

Tide pool
When the tide goes out, water is trapped in tide pools. Here, animals and plants can stay safely underwater.

Prawn · Starfish · Sponge · Sea-urchin

Seaweed
Seaweeds are plants that grip rocks with sticky pads. Their leaves are called fronds.

Shells
Shells of all shapes and sizes can be found on the seashore. Each shell was once home to a sea creature.

Seashore life

Pipefish have very long, thin bodies and hide in seaweed.

Crabs hide in holes in rocks and wave their pincer claws at their enemies.

Sea anemones can't move, but have stinging tentacles that kill their prey.

Seagulls eat almost anything, even dead fish on the beach.

The **goldsinny** is a tiny fish that lives only in tide pools.

Find out more > Australasia 26   Seas and oceans 124

World of Nature

Seasons

In many parts of the world there are different seasons in the year. The changes they bring affect most living things.

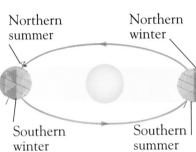

Northern summer
Northern winter
Southern winter
Southern summer

Earth and the seasons
We have seasons because the Earth tilts as it circles the Sun. When the north pole leans toward the Sun, it is summer in the north and winter in the south.

Four seasons
In many parts of the world, there are four seasons in the year.

Spring
The weather warms up. Plants begin to grow and many animals are born.

Trees grow new leaves.

Lambs are born.

Summer
The days are long and warm. Flowers bloom and fruits grow.

Butterflies feed on flowers.

Plants flower.

Trees are in full leaf.

Winter
Winter days are dark and cold. Little grows in the frozen soil.

Some trees have no leaves.

Some animals hibernate all winter.

It may often snow.

Fall
Fall days are shorter and cooler. Nuts and berries ripen in the woods.

Some trees start to lose their leaves.

Squirrels collect nuts for winter food.

Did you know?
The Arctic tern spends summer at the north pole, then flies all the way to the south pole for summer there!

Polar seasons
There are two seasons at the poles.

In summer, it is always light.

In winter, it is always dark.

Tropical seasons
There are two seasons in tropical areas – one wet and one dry.

For half the year, winds blow in from the sea, bringing heavy rains.

Find out more Climates 39 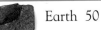 Earth 50

Science and Technology

Ships and boats

Anchor

Anchors act as brakes. They dig into the seabed and stop ships from moving.

Cruise ship

All boats do a particular kind of job. A cruise ship gives passengers a vacation at sea.

Ships and boats carry passengers and goods up and down rivers, over lakes, and from port to port across oceans and seas.

Rope

Ropes are used a lot on boats. Knots hold things in place.

The bridge is where the captain controls the ship from.

Portholes are cabin windows.

Lifeboat

Swimming pool

Anchor

Rudder for steering

Hull

Types of boats

Hovercraft float on a cushion of air. Fans blow air downward and lift the boat up.

Cargo ships carry containers full of goods around the world.

Trawlers are fishing boats. They drag a net that scoops up fish from the sea.

Frigates have missiles on board to strike enemy ships in times of war.

Did you know?

Cargo ships carry up to 2,700 containers. These would stack almost twice as high as Mount Everest!

Safety

All ships carry rescue equipment in case of accidents at sea.

Flares are like fireworks. They lead rescuers to where you are.

Life jackets help people float if they fall into the water.

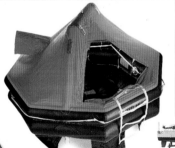

Life rafts are used to carry passengers if their boat sinks.

Moving in water

Different boats move in different ways.

Motorboats have an engine that turns a propeller.

Rowboats have oars to move them through the water.

Sailboats are driven by the wind.

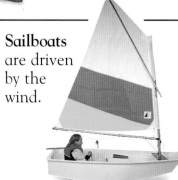

Paddle steamers go up and down rivers. They are driven by a wheel at the back.

Find out more ➤ Explorers 61   Transportation 142

World of Nature

Skeletons

A set of bones, an outer case, a beautiful shell – almost all animals have some sort of skeleton. Skeletons support the body and protect the soft parts inside.

Animal skeletons

Tortoises have an inner skeleton joined to their exoskeleton, or shell.

Elephant skull
The long tusks are actually teeth!

Long, light bones help the cat run faster.

Human skull
The large skull encloses a big brain.

Hips

Skull

Snakes can curl up because they have hundreds of bones in their spine.

Long, pointed teeth to kill prey

Long tail for balance

Spine is long and bendy

Cat skeleton
Without a skeleton, most animals, like this cat, would be floppy bags of skin with no shape!

Rib cage protects heart and lungs

Sharp claws to catch prey

Fish have long, bendy spines to help them move through water.

Birds have hollow bones, which make them light enough to fly in the air.

Exoskeleton
Many animals have a hard case or shell on the outside of their body. It is called an exoskeleton.

Beetle

Stiff plates make a hard casing that protects the beetle's soft body.

Shells
Some shells get bigger as the animal grows.

Shedding exoskeletons
As a crab grows, it gets too big for its shell. So it wriggles out of its old shell and grows a new, larger one.

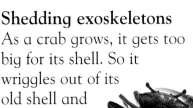

Did you know?
Worms have no bones at all. They are filled with fluid, which gives them their shape.

Frogs have short spines, but long back legs that are good for jumping.

Find out more ▷ Fossils 74   Human body: skeleton 82

Sound

The world is full of sounds. Some are useful, others are just annoying! But we hear them all in the same way.

Sound waves

All sounds are made by vibrations, which move the air and send out invisible sound waves to our ears.

Did you know?

Some singers can sing a note so high and so loud that it will shatter glass!

Sound waves move outward through the air.

Skin vibrates, or shakes.

Drum stick

Drum base

Warning sounds

Smoke detectors bleep loudly if a fire starts.

Alarm clocks ring to wake you in the morning.

Noise levels

The loudness of a sound is measured in decibels.

Falling leaves are quiet. Their noise measures 20 decibels.

Talking to people measures 30 to 60 decibels.

Vacuum cleaners reach 60 to 80 decibels.

Jumbo jets are very loud, making 140 decibels of noise!

Speed of sound

Light travels faster than sound. That is why you see lightning before you hear thunder.

Sound travels farther in water than in air. Whales can hear noise up to 60 miles (100 km) away.

Musical sounds

Musical instruments make sounds in different ways.

Recorders make sounds when air vibrates inside the hollow tube.

A **double bass** makes sounds as its strings vibrate.

South America

Central America and Caribbean

Central America's volcanoes, forests, and Caribbean sun-drenched islands are home to some exotic wildlife.

Pitch Lake
This lake in Trinidad is full of pitch – a black sticky tar in the ground.

Scarlet ibis
The ibis lives on the Caribbean islands. It pulls worms out of the mud with its long beak.

Volcano
On many of the islands, old volcanoes are covered by lush tropical rain forest.

Waterfall
The tropical islands have heavy rainfall. There are many spectacular waterfalls.

Coral reef
Coral reefs in warm Caribbean waters are home to sponges and tropical fish.

Bee hummingbird
Cuba is home to the world's smallest bird. Bee hummingbirds are the same size as a butterfly!

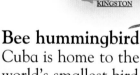

Passion flower
Passion flowers grow in climbing vines in the forests.

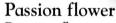

Beach
White, sandy beaches stretch their way around the shoreline. They are fringed with coconut palms.

Mangrove tree
These trees grow in wet, boggy land along many tropical coastlines.

Did you know?
- The Caribbean has some of the most dangerous storms in the world, called hurricanes.
- Hummingbirds are the only birds in the world that can fly backward!

Map labels:
NASSAU
HAVANA
CUBA
BAHAMAS
Greater Antilles
JAMAICA
KINGSTON
HAITI
PORT-AU-PRINCE
DOMINICAN REPUBLIC
SANTO DOMINGO
Virgin Islands
British Virgin Islands
SAN JUAN
Puerto Rico
Lesser Antilles
Antigua & Barbuda
Guadeloupe
Dominica
Martinique
St. Lucia
BARBADOS
ST. VINCENT AND THE GRENADINES
GRENADA
Netherlands Antilles
Aruba
PORT OF SPAIN
TRINIDAD & TOBAGO
BELIZE
BELMOPAN
GUATEMALA
GUATEMALA CITY
SAN SALVADOR
EL SALVADOR
HONDURAS
TEGUCIGALPA
NICARAGUA
MANAGUA
COSTA RICA
SAN JOSÉ
PANAMA
PANAMA CITY
N

Find out more

 Climates 39

 Mountains 99

Continents of the World

South America

South America
South America is home to the world's largest rain forest. It is bursting with color and is a refuge for rare plants and animals.

Did you know?
- The Amazon rain forest is more than 12 times the size of France.
- Lake Titicaca is the highest lake in the world.

Howler monkey
The screams of howler monkeys echo through the forest.

Amazon River
The Amazon and its surrounding rivers make up 20% of the world's freshwater.

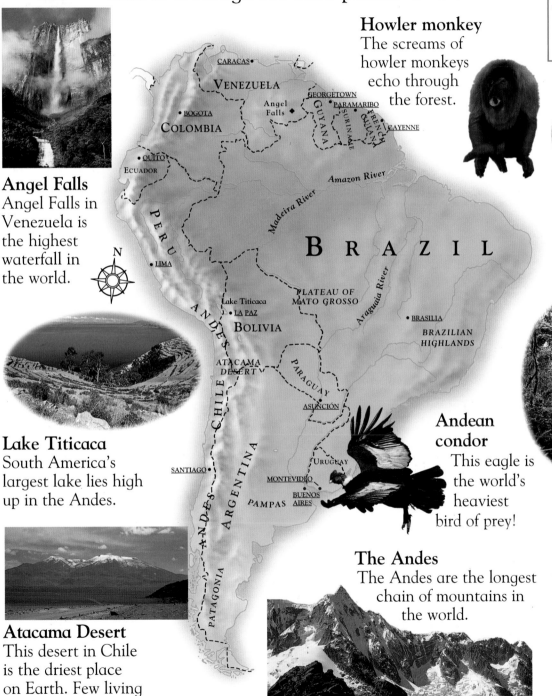

CARACAS

VENEZUELA

GEORGETOWN
Angel Falls ◆ PARAMARIBO
BOGOTA GUYANA SURINAME FRENCH GUIANA
COLOMBIA CAYENNE

QUITO
ECUADOR

Amazon River

Madeira River

B R A Z I L

PERU

N

LIMA

Lake Titicaca PLATEAU OF MATO GROSSO
LA PAZ Araguaia River
BOLIVIA BRASILIA
BRAZILIAN HIGHLANDS

ATACAMA DESERT PARAGUAY

CHILE ASUNCIÓN

URUGUAY

ANDES

SANTIAGO MONTEVIDEO
BUENOS AIRES
ARGENTINA PAMPAS

PATAGONIA

Angel Falls
Angel Falls in Venezuela is the highest waterfall in the world.

Rain forest
Rain forests are being cut down to make way for roads and industry.

Lake Titicaca
South America's largest lake lies high up in the Andes.

Andean condor
This eagle is the world's heaviest bird of prey!

Atacama Desert
This desert in Chile is the driest place on Earth. Few living things can survive here.

The Andes
The Andes are the longest chain of mountains in the world.

Pampas
The Pampas are the dry, rolling grasslands in Argentina. They are used for cattle grazing.

Find out more ➤ Birds of the world 31 Mountains 99

131

South America: culture

Continents of the World

Did you know ?
Panama hats are made from palm tree leaves that grow in Ecuador.

The people of Central and South America enjoy both modern and traditional lifestyles. There is a great variety of culture and customs.

Music
Music is very important to all South American cultures.

Steel drum

Guiro

Elaborate headdress

Brightly colored costume

Culture

Arts and crafts, such as jewelry making, still follow traditional methods.

Carnival, Brazil
Traditional festivals are still important today. Colorful dancers sway to modern music in this Brazilian carnival.

Brasilia
This cathedral lies in Brasilia, Brazil's capital city, which was built only 30 years ago.

Cricket is the most popular sport on the Caribbean Islands.

Christ the Redeemer
This statue stands high above Rio de Janeiro in Brazil.

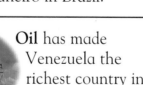

Food, like Italian pasta, has been introduced from other countries.

Industry

Oil has made Venezuela the richest country in South America.

Tourism is an important industry in South America. Many people flock to beaches there.

Copper mines in Chile are some of the largest in the world.

Steel works in Brazil produce the metal used to make cars.

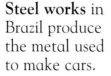

Ancient ruins of long-ago cities lie hidden in the forests of Central America.

Find out more Music 100 Trains 141

Science and Technology

Space travel

People have always wanted to know about space. For years scientists could only look up into the sky. Today, they can send up rockets to investigate.

Working in space
Astronauts leave the shuttle to do experiments.

Life in space

People float around in space because there is no gravity to hold them down.

Space shuttle
Astronauts inside the space shuttle are blasted into space on the back of a rocket.

Shuttle

Main fuel tank

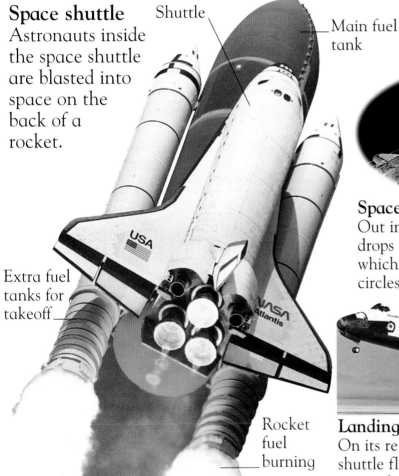

USA

NASA Atlantis

Extra fuel tanks for takeoff

Rocket fuel burning

Space orbit
Out in space, the rocket drops away from the shuttle, which then slowly orbits, or circles, the Earth.

Space suits are special protective outfits. They help astronauts breathe in space.

United States

Landing
On its return from space, the shuttle flies through the Earth's atmosphere and lands just like an ordinary plane.

Space food is different than normal food – it is dried to make it last.

SPACE FOOD

Viewing space
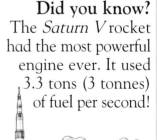

Satellite dishes on Earth collect information and pictures from satellites in space.

Satellites orbit in space. They send information back to Earth.

Space probes are sent into space to explore other planets.

Did you know?
The *Saturn V* rocket had the most powerful engine ever. It used 3.3 tons (3 tonnes) of fuel per second!

Spiders and mini-beasts

A spider in a corner, a snail in a wall, a worm underground – spiders and mini-beasts live all around us, but keep well hidden.

Web spider
A spider is not an insect. Insects have six legs. Spiders have eight.

The silk comes out of the spinnerets.

Webs
Web spiders make strong, sticky silk, which they spin into round orb webs to trap flying insects.

Two fangs grab prey.

Spiderlings
Baby spiders, called spiderlings, fly through the air on long pieces of silk.

This spider has eight eyes.

Each leg has six joints.

Abdomen

Mini-beasts

Centipedes can move fast. They feed on insects and slugs.

Millipedes have up to 400 legs. Most feed on rotting plants.

Sow bugs live where it's damp and shady. They feed on leaves.

Earthworms tunnel through soil, feeding on dead plants.

Scorpions kill their prey with the deadly sting on their tails.

Snails crawl along on their foot. They like to eat vegetables.

Did you know?
The pill millipede curls into a tight, solid ball when it's attacked by an enemy, such as a beetle or ant.

Hunting spiders
Not all spiders spin webs. Some hunt for food instead.

Chilean red-leg spiders eat mice and birds.

Trapdoor spiders ambush their unsuspecting prey.

Raft spiders can walk over ponds to find food.

Crab spiders kill insects with a poisonous bite.

Find out more Butterflies and moths 36   Insects 86

Sports

Life Today

Most people enjoy sports for the exercise and fun. But some people train hard to compete against the best athletes in the world.

Olympic Games
The Olympics are the world's greatest sports competition. They are held every four years.

Olympic medals
There are three medal winners in each event.

Olympic athletic stadium

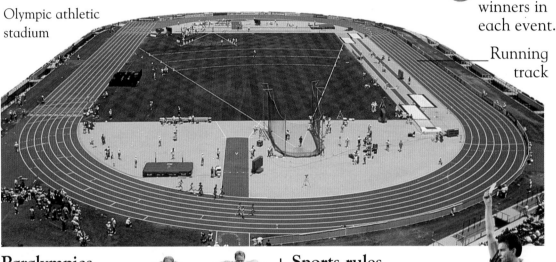

Running track

Sports events

The US Open is one of golf's great championships.

The **Cricket World Cup** is a competition between many nations.

The **Rugby World Cup** is a huge international tournament.

Paralympics
The Paralympics is an international competition for disabled athletes.

Sports rules
A referee or umpire makes sure players obey the rules. A blow on a whistle can stop a game.

Football referee

Winter Olympics
The Winter Olympics is a competition of winter sports, such as skiing and ice skating.

Whistle

Stopwatch

The **Formula 1 World Championship** is won by the fastest overall driver.

Sports gear
Each sport has special gear. Other pieces of equipment protect players from injury.

Baseball glove

Netball bib

Cricket pads

Ice-hockey helmet

Football sweater

The **Grand Slam** consists of four great tournaments in the tennis world.

Find out more   Human body: skin 83   Sports of the world 136

Sports of the world

All over the world, individual athletes train hard to compete among the best in their chosen sport.

Ice hockey

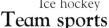
Baseball

Team sports
Most team sports are fast-moving ball games. The players in a team must work together to win.

Basketball

Attacker

Defender

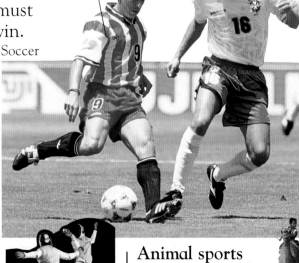
Soccer

Did you know?
The world's heaviest sumo wrestler weighs as much as four teenage boys.

Skiing

Individual sports
In some sports, people compete alone, trying to score points, or racing against the clock.

Gymnastics

One-on-one sports
In one-on-one sports, the players compete against one other person at a time.

Fencing

Animal sports
Horse racing is the best-known animal sport. But camels and other animals are raced, too.

Camel racing

Squash

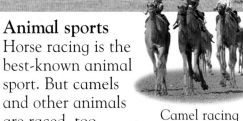
Horse racing

High jump

Water sports
Water sports take place on rivers, in the ocean, or in swimming pools indoors.

Surfing

Scuba diving

Swimming

Canoeing

Find out more North America: culture 105 Romans 121

Science and Technology

Sun and stars

Studying stars
Astronomers use different instruments to view the stars.

Telescopes offer the simplest way to look at the stars.

Observatories contain huge telescopes that can see many miles into space.

Space satellites send back pictures of stars to the Earth.

Huge groups of stars in space are called galaxies. The galaxy we live in is called the Milky Way. Our Sun is just one of millions of stars in the Milky Way.

Sun
Like all stars, the Sun is a huge ball of super-hot gas. It burns very brightly, giving Earth the heat and light it needs to support life.

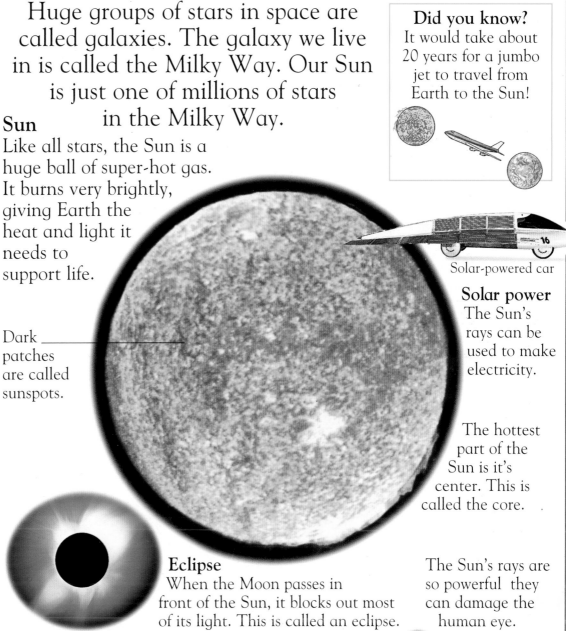

Dark patches are called sunspots.

Did you know?
It would take about 20 years for a jumbo jet to travel from Earth to the Sun!

Solar-powered car

Solar power
The Sun's rays can be used to make electricity.

The hottest part of the Sun is it's center. This is called the core.

The Sun's rays are so powerful they can damage the human eye.

Eclipse
When the Moon passes in front of the Sun, it blocks out most of its light. This is called an eclipse.

Mapping stars
On a clear night you can see thousands of stars in the sky. Astronomers have made maps of the stars.

Star map of the northern skies

Constellations
Groups of stars are called constellations. Each group is given a name.

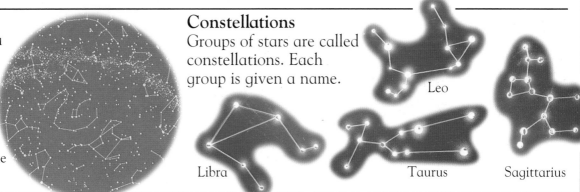

Leo

Libra

Taurus

Sagittarius

Television

Life Today

Television uses sound and moving pictures to broadcast sports, films, programs, and news from around the world.

Did you know?

The smallest television in the world is so tiny it can fit on a wrist-watch!

Television camera

Control room

People in the control room keep in close touch with the studio.

Television studio

Most TV programs are made inside with special lights and cameras. The large rooms are called studios.

On location

Some programs are made outside using smaller, lighter, cameras.

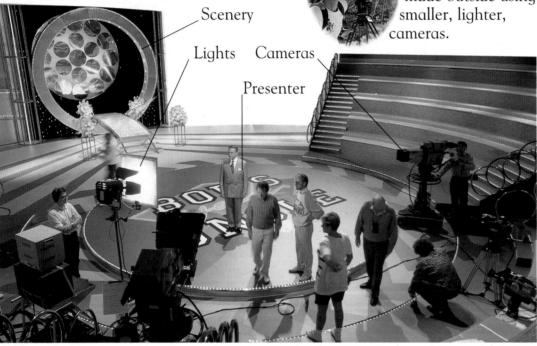

Scenery

Lights   Cameras

Presenter

TV programs

Movies are often shown on television.

News programs give daily reports and stories.

Documentaries, such as wildlife films, are programs about the real world.

Social events can be televised to reach wider audiences.

Children's programs are made to entertain and inform children.

How television works

1 Transmitters send out television signals as radio waves.

3 The television set turns the signals into sounds and pictures.

2 An antenna on the roof picks up the radio waves and sends signals to your

Satellite television

Some television signals are broadcast from satellites in space.

Satellite dish on roof

Find out more ⟩ Electricity at home 53   Film 66

Life Today

Theater

Types of plays

A **tragedy** is a serious play, with a sad ending.

Operas are plays performed by singers to music.

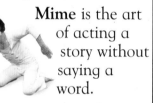

Mime is the art of acting a story without saying a word.

Comedies are funny plays, intended to make people laugh.

For thousands of years, people have enjoyed going to the theater for entertainment, watching actors perform.

Open-air theater
In some countries, theaters are built outdoors.

Theater building
The audience sits in rows on several different levels. The actors perform on a stage.

Downstairs is called the stalls.

Spotlight

Upstairs is called the balcony.

Chinese theater
In China, the costumes actors wear tell the audience about their characters.

Indian theater
Traditional Indian plays tell stories. The actors mime, sing, and dance.

Did you know?
The first theaters were built in Greece about 2,500 years ago.

Puppet theater
Glove, string, and shadow puppets are popular in theaters around the world.

Judy   Punch

Crocodile

Glove puppets, like Punch and Judy, are popular in Britain.

Shadow puppets are used in Southeast Asia.

Marionettes have up to 20 strings to move them.

Find out more   Film 66   Dance 44

Life Today

Towns and cities

Services

Office buildings are where many people work.

Hospitals can be big enough to treat thousands of patients.

Shopping is easy in a city. There are lots of big stores.

Schools are placed around a city for children of all ages.

Did you know?
The city of Venice, in Italy, is built on 108 islands. It has canals instead of roads!

Towns and cities are bustling places where thousands or millions of people live and work together.

City center
City centers are often built around a central square, where there are many historic buildings.

Skyscrapers
Tall skyscrapers save space on the ground, and form an exciting skyline.

Fountains   Old buildings

Transportation

Cable cars run on tracks and carry passengers up hills in some cities.

Buses are quick and easy for people traveling through the city streets.

Taxis are more expensive, but are useful for people who are in a hurry.

Ferries carry people along rivers and stop at many different landing points.

Entertainment
Cities have interesting places for people to visit or relax.

Parks are quiet, green spaces, away from busy streets.

Cafés are places to eat, drink, and watch the people passing by.

Museums and galleries have interesting objects and paintings to observe.

Find out more   Africa: culture 8   Homes and houses 78

Science and Technology

Trains

Types of trains

Breakdown trains clear fallen trees and broken trains off the tracks.

Crocodile trains pull cars up steep mountains. They can "bend" around corners.

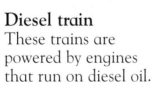

Shunters are mighty engines that push and pull other trains in a train yard.

Freight trains transport heavy loads across the country.

From the first puffing steam train to the electric "bullets" of today, trains have provided high-speed transportation for people and goods.

Electric train
Most of these are modern, high-speed passenger trains. They get their power from an electric cable above the track.

Electric cable

Did you know?
The first trains ran on tracks, but were pulled by horses!

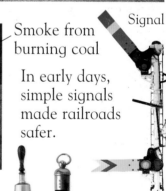
05
N C F

Diesel train
These trains are powered by engines that run on diesel oil.

Smoke from burning coal

Steam train
Early trains used the power of steam to drive their engines.

Signal

In early days, simple signals made railroads safer.

Bell   Whistle

City trains

Subway trains carry passengers under the busy city streets.

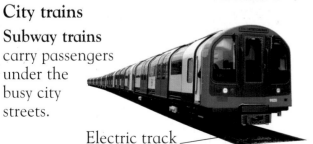

Electric track

Monorails run on a single track high above busy roads.

Magnetic levitation (maglev) trains float above a track. Strong magnets push the train into the air!

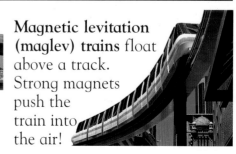

Transportation

Transportation of the world

Planes are a fast way to carry people and goods around the world.

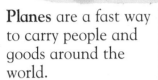

Tuk-tuks are small trucks used as taxis in Thailand.

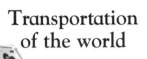

Bicycles are cheap and clean. They are popular in China.

Paddle steamers carry people up and down rivers.

Streetcars are electric buses, running on rails in some city centers.

People use all kinds of vehicles to travel long or short distances, and to carry heavy loads from place to place.

Different vehicles

New forms of transportation are being invented all the time, although some ancient forms are still in use.

A modern bullet train from Japan

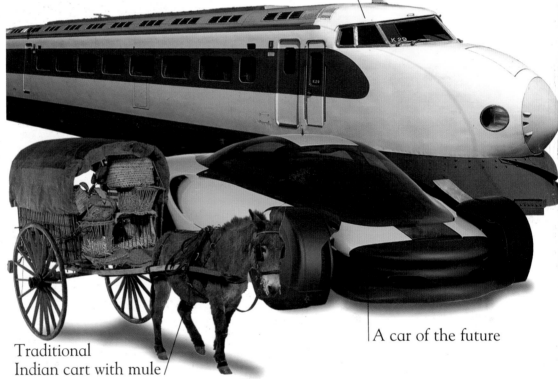

Traditional Indian cart with mule

A car of the future

Animals as transportation

Elephants in Asia carry very heavy loads. The driver is called a mahout.

Donkeys are very strong. They can carry people up steep mountain paths.

Camels are often called ships of the desert. They can carry goods and people in the heat.

Find out more Aircraft 10 Bicycles 29

Trees

Because of their size, it's easy to forget that trees are plants. But like any plant, they have roots, a stem, leaves, and flowers that make seeds.

Did you know?
The world's tallest tree is a coast redwood in North America. At 151 ft (111 m) it is taller than the Statue of Liberty in New York.

Oak tree
Every part of this deciduous oak tree helps it survive and grow.

Leaves
Leaves use sunlight, water, and air to make food for the tree.

Trunk
The trunk is the strong stem that sucks up food and water from the soil.

Leaves will drop off in the fall.

Branches, twigs, and leaves make up the crown of the tree.

Trunk

Acorns
Acorns are the seeds of the oak tree.

Roots grow under the ground.

Bark
The bark protects the trunk.

Tree products
Paper is made from mashed up wood.

Sculptures, such as totem poles, may be carved out of a whole tree trunk.

Maple syrup is made from the sweet juice, called sap, of sugar maples.

Furniture is made of wood from the trunks of trees.

Unusual trees

Bonsai trees are dwarf trees that are grown in pots.

Palm trees grow on sandy beaches.

Baobab trees survive in the desert by storing water in their trunks.

Mangrove trees grow in swamps. Their roots arch out over the water.

Find out more ➤ Forests 73   Rain forest animals 113

143

Trucks

Huge trucks rumble along our roads both night and day. Most carry goods around the country, but some are used for emergencies.

Types of trucks

Tankers carry liquid goods, such as oil, gasoline, or milk, around the country.

Street sweepers collect garbage from the streets and keep our towns clean.

Moving vans carry the furniture when people are moving to a new house.

Car carriers carry new cars from a factory to the showroom.

Snowplows have a large shovel at the front to clear snow from roads.

Semitrailer

This truck has two main parts – the cab at the front and the trailer at the back.

Engine under driver's cab

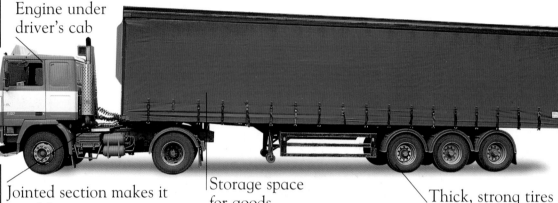

Jointed section makes it possible to turn corners.

Storage space for goods

Exhaust
Diesel fumes from the engine come out through the smokestack.

Inside a cab
Many large trucks have a bed in the cab so the driver can rest on long trips.

Thick, strong tires

Wheels
Trucks have lots of wheels to support their heavy loads.

Did you know?
The very first trucks were steam powered. Coal was shoveled into a boiler as the truck moved along!

Emergency trucks

Ambulances take people who are sick or hurt to the hospital.

Tow trucks take vehicles to a garage for repairs.

Fire engines carry firefighters, water pumps, and hoses to the scene of a fire.

Find out more  Building machines 34   Factories 62

Vikings

The Vikings from Scandinavia lived more than 1,000 years ago. They sailed all over Europe and America, fighting and trading.

Invading warrior
A Viking warrior attacked villagers on the coast.

Viking ships
The Vikings sailed great distances in strong, fast boats called longships.

Mast

Sail made of wool or linen

Single square sail

Room for 80 warriors

Snake-tail ornament

Rowing oar

Prowhead
The prowhead was a carving at the front of the ship.

Steering oar
This oar was used to steer the boat.

Prowhead

Steering oar

Metalwork

Bronze items, like this key, were often highly decorated.

Silver jewelry, like this brooch, was worn by wealthy people.

Iron shears were used to cut cloth and shear sheep for their wool.

Weather vanes sat on the masts of ships. They showed the wind direction.

Cooking pots made from iron or soapstone were hung over a fire.

Did you know?
Some Viking warriors prepared for battle by working themselves into a frenzy and going berserk. They were called berserkers!

Trade
The Vikings traveled far and wide, exchanging goods for gold and silver.

German glass cup

Coins

Scales to weigh goods

Weights for scales

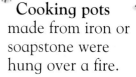

Find out more ➡ Explorers 61   Ships and boats 127

Science and Technology

Water

Dissolving
Some things seem to disappear when mixed with water. This is called dissolving.

Dirt dissolves in water. That is why you bathe!

Minerals in rocks can dissolve in water. They sometimes form stalactites in caves.

Oxygen dissolves in water. Fish need this oxygen to live.

Salts in rocks dissolve in water. They make seawater salty.

Water is the most important liquid on Earth. It has no smell, color, or taste, but without it people couldn't survive.

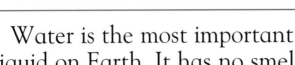

Water cycle
Water is always moving from the ocean, to the sky, to the land. This is called the water cycle.

3 River
The rain runs into rivers, which flow to the oceans.

Fastflowing stream

4 Ocean
The rivers empty their water into the ocean, and the cycle starts all over again.

Ice
Ice is so powerful it can cut huge valleys into hard rock.

1 Evaporation
The sun's heat turns water into water vapor. This rises, cools, and forms clouds.

2 Rain
Winds blow the clouds over land. Water in the clouds falls as rain, snow or hail.

Water for life
Every living thing needs water to survive.

Did you know?
The Dead Sea in Israel is so salty that people can sit up and float in it without sinking!

Forms of water
Water can change its form. It can be solid ice, a runny liquid, or steam – a gas that mixes with air.

Solid   Liquid   Gas

Find out more 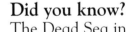 Living things 91 Seas and oceans 124

Weather

Wind, sun, rain, or snow – weather is what happens in the air around us. Weather affects our lives, so forecasts warn us when it will change.

Recording the weather

Anemometers spin around quickly. They measure the speed of wind.

Weather buoys gather information about all kinds of weather conditions.

Thermometers measure how hot or cold the air is.

Barometers are used to measure the pressure of air.

World weather
Satellites in space take pictures of the Earth. This one shows patterns of clouds around the globe.

Storm clouds

Rain clouds over the equator

Europe is sunny.

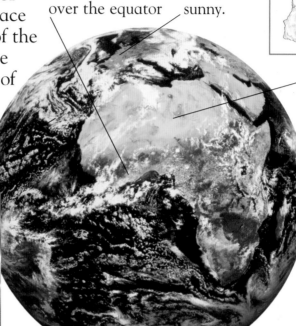

Clear skies over northern Africa

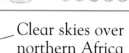

Did you know?
The biggest hailstone in the world fell in North America. It was as heavy as 13 tennis balls.

Snow
Rain turns to snow when the air is very cold.

Tornado
These strong, whirling winds twist at up to 300 mph (500 km/h).

Fog
Fog is a type of cloud that forms low down on the ground.

Rain

1 Clouds are made of tiny water droplets that float in the air.

2 The clouds get darker as more water droplets join together.

3 The droplets grow bigger and heavier until they fall to the ground as rain.

World map

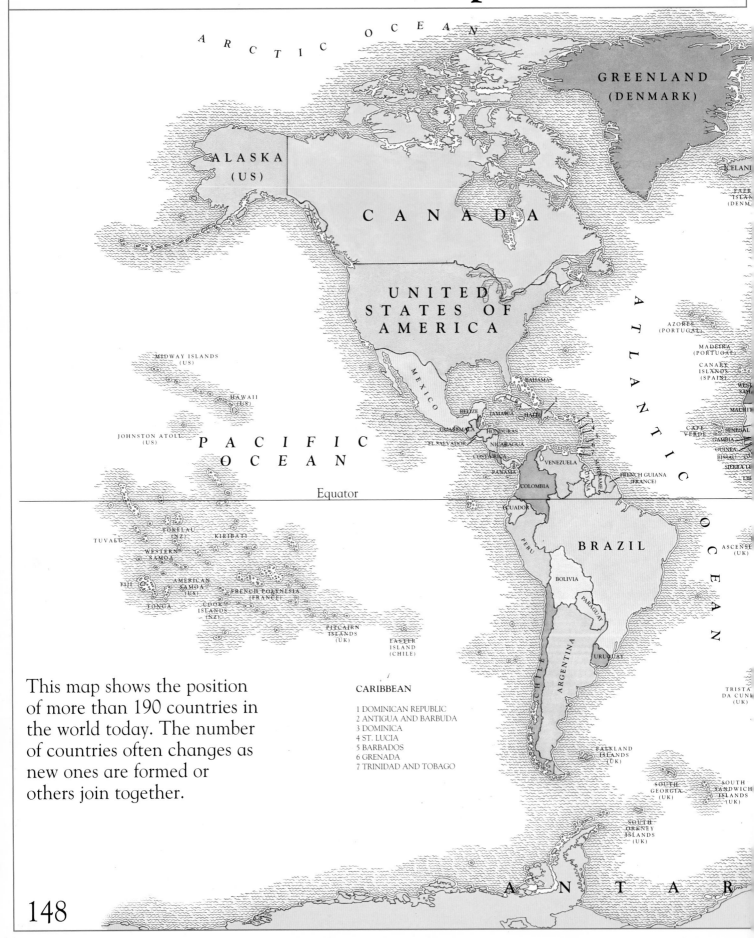

ARCTIC OCEAN

A R C T I C

GREENLAND
(DENMARK)

ICELAN

ALASKA
(US)

FAER
ISLAN
(DENM

C A N A D A

U N I T E D
S T A T E S O F
A M E R I C A

A
T
L
A
N
T
I
C

MIDWAY ISLANDS
(US)

AZORES
(PORTUGAL)

MEXICO

MADEIRA
(PORTUGAL)

HAWAII
(US)

BAHAMAS

CANARY
ISLANDS
(SPAIN)

WEST
SAH

BELIZE

JAMAICA

HAITI

JOHNSTON ATOLL
(US)

P A C I F I C
O C E A N

GUATEMALA

HONDURAS

EL SALVADOR

NICARAGUA

CAPE
VERDE

MADRIT

SENEGAL

GAMBIA

COSTA RICA

VENEZUELA

GUINEA
BISSAU

SIERRA LE

PANAMA

GUYANA

SURINAME

FRENCH GUIANA
(FRANCE)

LIB

COLOMBIA

Equator

ECUADOR

PERU

BRAZIL

ASCENSI
(UK)

TUVALU

TOKELAU
(NZ)

KIRIBATI

WESTERN
SAMOA

BOLIVIA

FIJI

AMERICAN
SAMOA
(US)

FRENCH POLYNESIA
(FRANCE)

PARAGUAY

TONGA

COOK
ISLANDS
(NZ)

PITCAIRN
ISLANDS
(UK)

EASTER
ISLAND
(CHILE)

URUGUAY

C
H
I
L
E

A
R
G
E
N
T
I
N
A

O
C
E
A
N

TRISTA
DA CUN
(UK)

This map shows the position
of more than 190 countries in
the world today. The number
of countries often changes as
new ones are formed or
others join together.

CARIBBEAN

1 DOMINICAN REPUBLIC
2 ANTIGUA AND BARBUDA
3 DOMINICA
4 ST. LUCIA
5 BARBADOS
6 GRENADA
7 TRINIDAD AND TOBAGO

FALKLAND
ISLANDS
(UK)

SOUTH
GEORGIA
(UK)

SOUTH
SANDWICH
ISLANDS
(UK)

SOUTH
ORKNEY
ISLANDS
(UK)

A N T A R

148

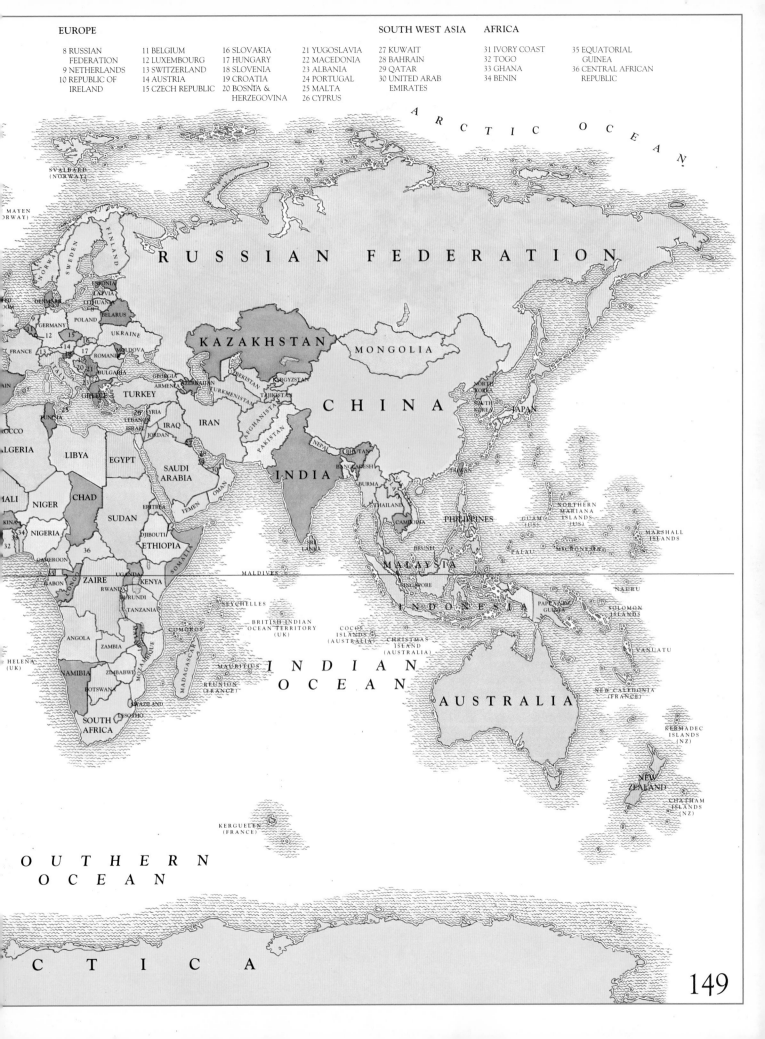

ARCTIC OCEAN

SVALBARD (NORWAY)

MAYEN (NORWAY)

RUSSIAN FEDERATION

NORWAY
SWEDEN
FINLAND
ESTONIA
LATVIA
LITHUANIA
DENMARK
GERMANY
POLAND
BELARUS
UKRAINE
FRANCE
MOLDOVA
ROMANIA
BULGARIA
ITALY
GEORGIA
ARMENIA
AZERBAIJAN
GREECE
TURKEY
UZBEKISTAN
KYRGYZSTAN
TURKMENISTAN
TAJIKISTAN
SYRIA
LEBANON
ISRAEL
JORDAN
IRAQ
IRAN
AFGHANISTAN
PAKISTAN

KAZAKHSTAN

MONGOLIA

CHINA

NORTH KOREA
SOUTH KOREA
JAPAN

NEPAL
BHUTAN
INDIA
BANGLADESH
BURMA
TAIWAN
THAILAND
SRI LANKA
CAMBODIA
PHILIPPINES

NORTHERN MARIANA ISLANDS (US)
GUAM (US)
MARSHALL ISLANDS
PALAU
MICRONESIA

MOROCCO
ALGERIA
TUNISIA
LIBYA
EGYPT
SAUDI ARABIA
OMAN
YEMEN
ERITREA
CHINA
MALI
NIGER
CHAD
SUDAN
NIGERIA
DJIBOUTI
ETHIOPIA
36
CAMEROON
35
GABON
CONGO
ZAIRE
UGANDA
KENYA
SOMALIA
RWANDA
BURUNDI
TANZANIA
SEYCHELLES

BRUNEI
MALAYSIA
SINGAPORE
INDONESIA
NAURU
PAPUA NEW GUINEA
SOLOMON ISLANDS

MALDIVES

BRITISH INDIAN OCEAN TERRITORY (UK)

COCOS ISLANDS (AUSTRALIA)

CHRISTMAS ISLAND (AUSTRALIA)

VANUATU

ANGOLA
ZAMBIA
COMOROS
MOZAMBIQUE
MADAGASCAR
MAURITIUS
REUNION (FRANCE)

HELENA (UK)

INDIAN OCEAN

NAMIBIA
ZIMBABWE
BOTSWANA
SWAZILAND
LESOTHO
SOUTH AFRICA

NEW CALEDONIA (FRANCE)

AUSTRALIA

KERMADEC ISLANDS (NZ)

KERGUELEN (FRANCE)

NEW ZEALAND

CHATHAM ISLANDS (NZ)

OUTHERN OCEAN

CTICA

149

World map: continents

This world map shows all seven continents. Each continent, except for Antarctica, is made up of several countries.

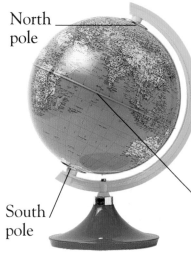

North pole

South pole

Globe
A globe is a round map of the world. The Earth spins around an invisible pole, called the north pole at the top and the south pole at the bottom.

The equator is an imaginary line that divides the Earth in half.

North America
North America stretches from the North pole almost to the equator.

Europe
This is one of the smallest continents, but it has one of the largest populations.

Asia
Asia is the largest continent, with the largest population.

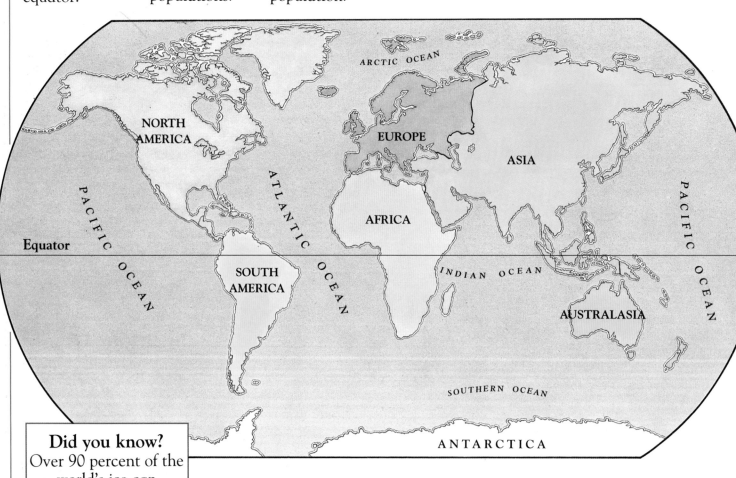

ARCTIC OCEAN

NORTH AMERICA

EUROPE

ASIA

PACIFIC OCEAN

ATLANTIC OCEAN

AFRICA

Equator

SOUTH AMERICA

INDIAN OCEAN

PACIFIC OCEAN

AUSTRALASIA

SOUTHERN OCEAN

ANTARCTICA

Did you know?
Over 90 percent of the world's ice can be found in the continent of Antarctica.

South America
The continent of South America stretches all the way from the equator almost to the south pole.

Africa
Africa is the second largest continent. The equator runs through the center of it.

Australasia
This area includes Australia, which is the smallest continent, and many other small islands.

Antarctica
This is the coldest and most southerly continent. No one lives here permanently.

Canada

Canada	
Capital city:	Ottawa
Country area:	9,970,610 sq km (3,849,562 sq miles)
Population:	29,953,000
Longest river:	River Mackenzie 4,241 km (2,635 miles)
Highest mountain:	Mount Logan 5,959 m (19,551 ft)

Canada is the second largest country in the world. It is an important nation and one of the richest in the world.

Farming
Wheat farming dominates the landscape, especially in the Central Plains or Prairies.

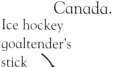

National Park
This beautiful national park in Banff is the oldest in Canada.

Canada's national flag

Royal Canadian Mounted Police
This police force is the oldest and most famous in Canada.

Lacrosse ball

Ice hockey goaltender's stick

Lacrosse stick

Ice hockey puck

Sport
Lacrosse
Ice Hockey
Baseball
Curling

YUKON TERRITORY

NORTHWEST TERRITORRIES

NEWFOUNDLAND

PRINCE EDWARD ISLAND

BRITISH COLUMBIA

ALBERTA

MANITOBA

SASKATCHEWAN

ONTARIO

QUEBEC

NOVA SCOTIA

NEW BRUNSWICK

OTTAWA

Niagara Falls

Parliament
The government of Canada runs the country but the Queen is still the reigning monarch.

Niagara Falls
Its two stunning waterfalls thunder across the U.S./Canadian border.

Industry
Wood is pulped in mills, like this one in Vancouver, to make paper.

World history timeline

This timeline lists some of the important events in world history and shows when they happened.

Early people begin to make tools from stones.

30,000 BC

Flint arrow-head

Hieroglyphs
Ancient Egypt is at the height of its power.

3,000

Jesus Christ is crucified about this time.

AD 1   30

Emperor Augustus

The **Roman Empire** grows across Europe.

100

Roman soldier

Christianity becomes the official religion of the Roman Empire.

391

Mayan statue

Mayan civilization develops in Central America.

600

The **plague** kills one-third of Europe's population.

1347–1351

The **Aztec and Inca empires** grow in Central and South America.

Statue of a llama

1350–1519

The **first printed book** in Europe – the Bible – is made in Germany.

1455

The **Renaissance** brings great changes to life in Europe. It is a time of learning in science and art.

Painting by Leonardo da Vinci

1450–1600

The **English Civil War** ends and King Charles I is executed.

The execution of Charles I

1649

Peter the Great becomes ruler of Russia. He improves industry and education.

1682

The **Revolutionary War** ends British rule in the US.

1775–1783

George Washington becomes the first president of the US.

1789

Canada becomes independent from Britain.

1867

The first **automobile** is invented by the German Karl Benz.

1898 Benz "Velo"

1885

English hunting in India

The **British Empire** is at its peak.

1804–1885

Australia gains independence from Britain.

1901

The first successful **airplane flight** is made by American Orville Wright.

1903

Australia welcomes about 2 million settlers from Europe.

1945

Gandhi leads the movement for Indian independence from Britain.

1947

Mao Tse-tung makes China a communist republic.

Germany is split into West Germany and communist East Germany.

1949

Mount Everest, the world's highe[st] mountain, is climbed by Edmund Hillary and Sherpa Tenzing Norgay.

1953

Judaism spreads throughout western Asia.

Star of David

2,000

Ancient Greek civilization is at its peak. The Parthenon is built in Athens.

Greek vase

500

Buddhism starts in India with the birth of its founder, Siddhartha Gautama.

563

The **Chinese Empire** begins when Shih Juang-ti unites China, and becomes its first emperor.

Shih Juang-ti

221

The prophet **Muhammed** begins the religion of Islam.

622

Vikings from Scandinavia travel widely to find new lands and trading partners.

Viking longship

800

Christian Crusaders from Europe fight to regain control of Jerusalem from the Muslims.

Crusaders

1096–1291

Italian-born **Christopher Columbus** crosses the Atlantic Ocean.

Astrolabe

1492

The **world is round**, not flat. This was discovered by Spanish explorers.

1500

Japan stops all contact with foreigners and the outside world for the next 200 years.

1639

The **slave trade** grows. Many Africans are seized and shipped to America.

1600–1800

The **French Revolution** brings down the monarchy in France.

1789

Steam trains are invented. They are powered by wood or coal.

1830

Maori rebellion in New Zealand ends British rule. New Zealand is allowed to govern itself.

1850

Civil War breaks out between the states of America. Slaves are set free.

1861

World War I is fought in Europe.

1914–1918

The **Russian Revolution** overthrows the Tzar. Lenin becomes the new communist leader.

Vladimir Illich Lenin

1917

The **Great Depression** is a time of great hardship in the US.

1929

World War II breaks out after German leader Hitler invades Poland.

British fighter plane

1939–1945

The **Vietnam War** is fought. American troops help South Vietnam.

1965–1973

Neil Armstrong is the first person to walk on the Moon.

1969

The **Berlin Wall** comes down as East and West Germany reunite.

1989

Nelson Mandela becomes president of South Africa.

1994

153

Index of entries

Acknowledgments

Additional editorial assistance Stella Love and Susan Peach

Additional design assistance Peter Radcliffe and Cheryl Telfer

Additional picture research Garifalia Boussiopoulou and Tom Worsley

Index Hilary Bird

Cartography Roger Bullen

Jacket design Sophia Tampakopoulos

Additional illustrations

Angelika Elsebach, John Hutchinson, Ruth Lindsay, Daniel J Pyne, Gill Tomblin, John Woodcock, Colin Woolf.

Photography

Peter Anderson, Sarah Ashen, Jane Burton, Paul Bricknell, Geoff Brightling, Peter Chadwick, Andy Crawford, Geoff Dann, Philip Dowell, Mike Dunning, Andreas Von Einsiedel, Neil Fletcher, Lynton Gardiner, Max Gibbs, Steve Gorton, Frank Greenway, Bob Guthany, Alan Hills, Michael Holford, Colin Keates, Gary Kevin, Barnabas Kindersley, Dave King, Bob Laneirish, C. Laubscher, Richard Leeny, Ruth Lindsay, Mike Linley, Andrew McRobb, Tony Morrison, David Murray, Martin Norris, Stephen Oliver, Roger Philips, Tim Ridley, Dave Rudkin, Saville Garden (Windsor), James Stephenson, Karl Shone, Steve Shott, James Stevenson, Clive Streeter, Harry Taylor, Kim Taylor, Peter Visscher, Barrie Watts, Matthew Ward, Steven Wooster, Jerry Young, Michael Zabe.

Picture agency credits

The publisher would like to thank the following for their kind permission to reproduce the photographs:
t=top, c=center, b=bottom, r=right, l=left, a=above.

Ancient Art & Architecture: R. Sheridan 13bcr, J.P. Stevens 13bc.
Aerofilms: 121tr.
Allsport: S. Bruty 135c, P. Cole 135cl, C. Cole 135cr, M. Cooper 136bcr, M. Hewitt 135cr, A. Murrell 132, D. Pensinger 136crb, G.M. Prior 135crb, B. Radford 135cra, P. Roudean 135cr, R. Stewart 103cra, 136tr, cra, cr.
Ardea: G. Behrens 119cb, L. Bomford 15br, F. Gohier 45c, E. Haagner 15cra, C. Haanger 15cra, P. Morris 75bc, 67bc, P. Steyn 15crb, J. Swedberg 30tl / 15cr, br, 19br, 130ca, 130tr, 119bc, 118cla.
Barnaby's Picture Library: 34c / B. Gibbs 33c, 33clb.
BBC Natural History Unit: Phil Chapman 19ca.
Bildarchiv Foto Marburg: 89tc.
BMW GB Ltd: 57cb.
Bridgman Art Library: 115c, crb.
British Library: 32cla.
British Antarctic Survey: 19bc.
Bruce Coleman: 15bc, 19cl, crb, 20clb, 24bc, 58tr, cb, cl, 60crb, 76cr, 96c, cr, 102c, 102crb, 104 cb, 110cb, 115c, 122bl, 130cla, cb, 146cr / E&P Bauer 111cr, J. Burton 134tc, J. Cancalosi 104c, E. Chrichton 24cla, G. Cubitt 21cla, 7tc, R. Forest 39cl, K. Gunnar 99br, T.O. Hounsen 60clb, J. Johnson 76c, H. Kranawetter 115cra, O. Langrand 105tc, A. Manzannres 15cb, Charlie Ott 112tr, Andy Prue 16bc, Hans Reinhard 20br, 27cl, 68cl, K. Rujhby 27cr, Kim Taylor 143br, U. Walz 119c, Konrad Wothe 143bc, J. Worrall 52clb, C. Zuber 75bl.
BT Corporate Pictures: 42cr.
Cadbury Ltd: 62c.
Central Broadcasting: 138c, tc, cra.
Collections: Patrich Wise 121cl.
Colorific: Steve Razzetti 24bc / 71br.
The Colour Museum, Bradford: 40bl.
Donald Cooper: 139c.
Corbis Bettman: 62tr.
Lupe Cunha: 79tr, c.
James Davis: 20cl.
Environmental Images: 23cb.
ET Archive: 121crb.
Eye Ubiquitous: 59bl / 147tl Chris Rose.
Fiat: 132bc.
Ronald Grant Archive: 66bl, crb, tr, cra.
Robert Harding: 7crb, tr, 9bc, 10tc, c, 19cla, 24bl, 25crb, tr, bl, 26tl, 28bc, tr, 32c, 39bl, 44cl, 55br, 56cr, 60cr, tr, 65cra, cb, 71bl, 78bc, cl, cra, 103br, 104ca, 105clb, cra, 115bl, bc, br, 130cl, 132cb, 140c, 148tr, cla, tl, bc / G. Hoberman 113c, cr, A. Tovy 12c, Dr T. Waltham 103cb.
Paul Harris: 102cb, crb.
Michael Holford: 38clb, 61cb.
Holiday Film Corp: 98cb.
Holt Studios: Nigel Cattlin 21clb.
House and Interiors: 106tl.
Hulton Getty: 19clb.
The Hutchison Library: 13tc, 23br, 44bl, 56cb, 85 br, cr, 93 cra, 103ca / N. Froggatt 56cra, ND Kenna 71cla, A. Tully 56bc.
ICCE: 7cla C. Aveling.
Image Bank: 6tr, 20cla, 24tl, clb, 28cra, 32bc, 33bc, 44br, 51cla, bl, 52crb, cb, c, 62ca, cra, cr, crb, br, bl, 65bcr, tr, 78cb, cr, 79cl, c, 90cr, 98br, 99bc, 100crb, cra, c, 114crb, 122cl, cla, tl, c, 124clb, bl, 126cra, cr, cb, 136bc, 138cra, bl, 142bc, 146cla, c / S. Allen 133bcr, A. Becker 59ca, PG Bowater 106cb, 63cr, D. Brownell 104tl, L. Gatz 41tr, Kay Churnogh 81tr, W. Clark 60crb, L. Castenada 140tl, David de Lossy 91bl; L. Dennis 58clb, W. Dietrech 38br, P. Doherty 88bl, 34bl, P. Eden 140cla, L. Gatz 41tr, J. Gocia 45c, Grant V. Faint 57br,

91br; J. Freis 71bc, M. Holford 63bl, J. Hunter 43bc, 90br, D&L King 124cl, C. Koher 43cl, R. Kristofik 98br, F. Lemmens 131cl, P. McCoirivelle 126cla, A. Meyerson 63br, P. Miller 119tr, S. Nierdorf 142cla, P. Peret 146ca, 28br A. Pistolesi, T. Rakke 58cb, D. Redfern 106tr, 138bcl, M. Rietz 151cr, Barrie Rokeach 98bc, G.A. Rossi 20cra; T. Schmitt 39cb, bc, H. Schon 71cra, G. M. Smith 56ca, G. Sund 77tl, H. Sund 105br, P. Turner 90cb, J. Van Os 102cla, 63tr, 72bc, 85c, Jurgen Vogt 103c, M. Wang 64ca, F. Whitney 78c, S. Wilkinnson 35br, A. T. Willett 129bl, K. Wothe 77c, L.F. Browne 90cra.

Images Colour Library: 41br, 52tr, 60c.
The Kobal Collection: 66cb, 138tr.
Mark A. Leman: 106bc.
FLPA: 52br, 60br, 96cra / E&D Hosking 27cra, G. Moon 27br.
Magnum Photos: Steve Mcmurray 126br / 24tr.
The Met Office: 47cla.
Microsoft: 42c.
John Cleare / Mountain Camera: John Cleare 9cb, 40c, 119ca, 126bl.
Natural History Museum: 48crb, 128ca / C. Keates 36bc, Dave King 128c.
Peter Newark's Historical Pictures: 49tr.
NHPA: 19bl, 146bc, 90cra, tr / K. Aitken 91bc, Laurie Campbell 9cra, M. Whendler 15bl.
Only Horses: 59c.
Oxford Scientific Films: 130cr / D. Bromhall 80cla, B. P. Kent 118bl.
Panos: 6cla, 8bc, 100cb, 131clb / Neil Cooper 24tl, Alainle Garsmeur 7cr, J. &L. Lythgoe 131cr.
Pictor: 6cla, cr, cb, bcr, 7cb, 20tr, bc, crb, ca, 24br, clb, 26br, 28br, 34bc, 44c, 54c, 57ca, cl, br, 60c, 119bc, 124cb, ca, clb, 141bc, c, 142ca, 146clb, cl.
Planet Earth Pictures: 6bcr, 15c, 20ca, 119clb, 124cb, ca, 146cl / Gary Bell 124cb, K. A. Puttock 39cr.
Popperfoto: 65tl.
QA Photos: 33bc, br.
Redferns: 44cla, cb, 105crb, cr.
Rex: 23c, bc, 44crb, 54bc, 55bc, 56bc, 65cl, 66br, 92bc, 102cr, 107cla, 112c, 113c, cr, 132 cb, 138bl, br, 139cl, 148cb, cl.
Royal Tyrell Museum: 48ca, cra.
Scala: 14tl.
Science Photo Library: 50cl, 74tl, 87clb, 98tl, crb, A. Bartel 141bc, P. Bassett 137cl, Dr. J. Burgess 84cl, Space Telescope Science Institute 109cra.
Shout: 79bc, cra.
Skyscan Photo Library: 146c.
Solar Wings: 9tr.
South American Pictures: 131cra / Robert Francis 132bl, T. Morrison 85ca, tr, 132crb, br, Space Telescope Science Institute/NASA 109cra.
Spectrum: 38cr, crb, 58cra, CNRI 83ca, M. Dohrn 9clb, K. Edward 84ca, G. Garradd 40cl, Manfred Kage 82c, John Mead 133bl, D. Millar 19cra, H. Morgan 84bl, NASA 93bl, cl, 109tr, bl, bc, 133ca, bc, cl, tc, tr; Alfred Pasie

84ca, Philippe Plailly 84bc, Revd R. Royer 137cb, US Geological Survey 109c, Frank Zullo 137tl.
Harry Smith Collection: 114cl, clb.
Sporting Pictures: 58clb, 135clb, 136cla, c, bl, crb, cl, cb;
Stock Photos: 138bc / U. E. Wallin 10cra.
Syndicated Truck Features: 144c, cb.
Telegraph Colour Library: 21ca, 52bl.
Tony Stone Images: 7clb, cra, cb, c, 13c, 25 br, 33cl, 35bc, 44tl, 55clb, crb, ca, 63bc, c, 65c, cr, 66crb, 72c, 79cla, bl, br, crb, 80clb, 97clb, 100cl, 102cl, 105bc, tr, 107c, 111c, 139c, 142br, 146bc, tr, 147bc / G. Allison 33bl, D. Armand 141bc, 26bl, D. Austen 26cla, H. Baender 103clb, O. Benn 130bl, T. Brase 147br, M. Brooke 27br, R. Bullard 147c, M. Busselle 57ca, 72ca, J. Calder 12bcr, A. Cassidy 56c, T. Cazabon 12br, P. Chesley 27bl, bc, S. Climpson 131bc, C. Condina 35tr, P. Correz 41ca, D. Cox 72bl, R. Dahlquist 27ca, N. de Vore 8bc, 24cr, S. Ellis 108cl, D. H. Endersbee 58c, R. Everts 60crb, br, 99c, B. Filet 111br, S&N Geary 25c, 63c, M. Goway 8c, L. Grandadan 60c, N. Gunderson 64tr, C. Gupton 21c, D. Hames 35crb, C. Harvey 8cra, A. Husmo 68bc, S. Jawncey 43cla, G. Johnson 35c, D. Johnston 37tcr, J. Kapec 102br, P. Kenward 27clb, M. Kezar 8cla, C. Krebbs 73bc, B. Krist 97crb, J. Lamb 14tr, 27c, crb, P. & S. Lamberti 119cr, J. Lawlor 105cra, M. Leman 106bc, cr, Y. Marcoux 147cr, M. Mcqueen 47bc, I. Murphy 8cb, J. Nelson 12cr, L. Nishevich 140tc, F. Prenzel 35cra, E. Pritchard 142cl, P. Redman 140cl, RNHRD NHS Trust: 88cra, M. Rosenfield 97cb, A. Sacks 105cr, 97clb, D. Saunders 28c, K. Schafer 111c, I. Shaw 60cl, H. Sitton 25cl, R. Smith 26clb, 148bc, J. Strachan 28crb, N. Snowdon 54c, O. Strewe 148tc, R. Talbot 39tr, 97c, D. Torcklev 129bc, P. Tweddie 28bc, C. Waite 59cla, 64cb, P. Ward 28cb, J. Warden 93br, 102bl, 64cb, R. Wells 104bc, cr, K. Westerkov 111ca, A. Wolfe 26cr, D. Woodfall 43c, tcr, 148bl, G. Yeowell 142cb, T. Zimmerman 44cra.
Topham Picturepoint: 65bl.
D. Torckler: 129bc.
Trip: H. Sayer 130cra, J. Short 130tr, 148ca, cr, bl.
The Wallace Collection: 89c.
Werner Forman Archive: 61cla.
Yamaha: 29cb.
Zefa: 6cra, clb, 7cl, 8bl, 9c, 10bl, bc, 12bc, 26cl, cb, cra, 28ca, 32br, 33cla, tl, 35bc, 41bc, 43ca, 50cra, 52cr, 64tl, cr, 74br, bc, 78cb, cra, br, crb, 83tr, 100cla, bc, 101cl, 104clb, crb, 105cl, bl, br, 112tc, 118clb, cl, 129cr, 131cla, 132c, clb, 135ca, 138crb, 142bl, 146bc, 147cb, cl, 148bc, cr / K. Goebel 119br, N. Holt 34crb, W. Mahl 34c, M. Mehltretter 141bl, Dr. Mueller 9ca.
Zen Radovan: 115br, 146clb.

Every effort has been made to trace the copyright holders. DK apologizes for any unintentional omissions and would be pleased, in such cases, to add an acknowledgment in future editions.